Apress Pocket Guides

Apress Pocket Guides present concise summaries of cutting-edge developments and working practices throughout the tech industry. Shorter in length, books in this series aims to deliver quick-to-read guides that are easy to absorb, perfect for the time-poor professional.

This series covers the full spectrum of topics relevant to the modern industry, from security, AI, machine learning, cloud computing, web development, product design, to programming techniques and business topics too.

Typical topics might include:

- A concise guide to a particular topic, method, function or framework

- Professional best practices and industry trends

- A snapshot of a hot or emerging topic

- Industry case studies

- Concise presentations of core concepts suited for students and those interested in entering the tech industry

- Short reference guides outlining 'need-to-know' concepts and practices.

More information about this series at https://link.springer.com/ bookseries/17385.

Task Programming in C# and .NET

Modern Day Foundation for Asynchronous Programming

Vaskaran Sarcar

Apress®

Task Programming in C# and .NET: Modern Day Foundation for Asynchronous Programming

Vaskaran Sarcar
Kolkata, West Bengal, India

ISBN-13 (pbk): 979-8-8688-1278-1   ISBN-13 (electronic): 979-8-8688-1279-8
https://doi.org/10.1007/979-8-8688-1279-8

Managing Director, Apress Media LLC: Welmoed Spahr
Acquisitions Editor: Smriti Srivastava
Coordinating Editor: Kripa Joseph

Cover designed by eStudioCalamar

Distributed to the book trade worldwide by Apress Media, LLC, 1 New York Plaza, New York, NY 10004, U.S.A. Phone 1-800-SPRINGER, fax (201) 348-4505, e-mail orders-ny@springer-sbm.com, or visit www.springeronline.com. Apress Media, LLC is a California LLC and the sole member (owner) is Springer Science + Business Media Finance Inc (SSBM Finance Inc). SSBM Finance Inc is a **Delaware** corporation.

For information on translations, please e-mail booktranslations@springernature.com; for reprint, paperback, or audio rights, please e-mail bookpermissions@springernature.com.

Apress titles may be purchased in bulk for academic, corporate, or promotional use. eBook versions and licenses are also available for most titles. For more information, reference our Print and eBook Bulk Sales web page at http://www.apress.com/bulk-sales.

Any source code or other supplementary material referenced by the author in this book is available to readers on GitHub (https://github.com/Apress/Task-Programming-in-C-and-.NET). For more detailed information, please visit https://www.apress.com/gp/services/source-code.

If disposing of this product, please recycle the paper

*To my seniors, colleagues, and teachers including C#
and .NET community members who directly
and indirectly helped me to write better code.
In fact, I am still learning from them.*

Table of Contents

TABLE OF CONTENTS

About the Author

 **Vaskaran Sarcar** obtained his Master of Engineering degree in Software Engineering from Jadavpur University, Kolkata (India), and an MCA from Vidyasagar University, Midnapore (India). He was a National Gate Scholar (2007–2009) and has over 12 years of experience in education and the IT industry. He devoted his early years (2005–2007) to the teaching profession at various engineering colleges, and later, he joined HP India PPS R&D Hub in Bangalore. He worked there until August 2019 and became a Senior Software Engineer and Team Lead. After working for more than ten years at HP, he decided to follow his passion completely. He is now an independent full-time author.

You can refer to the link amazon.com/author/vaskaran_sarcar (or Appendix B) to find all his books. You can also find him on LinkedIn at https://www.linkedin.com/in/vaskaransarcar.

About the Technical Reviewer

Shekhar Kumar Maravi is a software architect – design and development, whose main interests are programming languages, Linux system programming, Linux kernel, algorithms, and data structures. He obtained his master's degree in Computer Science and Engineering from Indian Institute of Technology Bombay. After graduation, he joined Hewlett Packard's R&D Hub in India to work on printer firmware. Currently, he is a Product and Solution Development Team Lead for automated pathology lab diagnostic devices at Siemens Healthcare R&D division. He can be reached by email at shekhar.maravi@gmail.com or via LinkedIn at https://www.linkedin.com/in/shekharmaravi.

Acknowledgments

At first, I thank the Almighty. I sincerely believe that with His blessings only, I could complete this book. I extend my deepest gratitude and thanks to the following people:

> **Shekhar**: Whenever I was in need, he provided support. He answered all my queries over phone calls, WhatsApp, and emails. Thank you one more time.

> **Smriti, Kripa, Celestin, and the Apress team**: I sincerely thank each of you for giving me another opportunity to work with you and Apress.

> **Nirmal and the Production team**: Thanks to each of you for your exceptional support in beautifying my work. Your efforts are extraordinary.

Finally, I thank those people from different online communities (particularly, the C# developer community, .NET developer community, and Stack Overflow community) who share their knowledge in various forms. In fact, I thank everyone who directly or indirectly contributed to this work.

Introduction

With the availability of multicore computers, asynchronous programming and parallel programming are becoming increasingly important. Why not? It is essential for building highly responsive software.

This is why playing with threads in a multithreaded environment is inevitable. Undoubtedly, it is hard, but in earlier days, it was harder. To simplify the overall coding experience, starting from the .NET Framework 4.0, Microsoft introduced Task Parallel Library (TPL) which was based on the concept of tasks. Later, in C#5, we saw the revolutionary introduction of the `async` and `await` keywords. Using them, we started passing the heavy work(s) to the compiler. However, you need to remember that a typical `async` method normally returns a task (in programming terms, a `Task` or a `Task<TResult>`). So, there is no wonder that task programming became the modern-day foundation for asynchronous programming. In addition, the patterns used earlier to deal with asynchronous and parallel programming are not recommended now.

This is why I decided to write a pocketbook series on asynchronous and parallel programming. This pocketbook series will try to simplify the concept using the modern C# features and libraries that Microsoft recommends. *Task Programming in C# and .NET: Modern Day Foundation for Asynchronous Programming* is the first book in this series. It focuses on task programming without using the `async` and `await` keywords.

How Is the Book Organized?

This book helps you to understand task programming using six chapters with many Q&A sessions and exercises. To give you an idea about the organization of the chapters and the contents of this book, let me summarize the following points:

- Chapter 1 introduces asynchronous programming with useful scenarios. It also provides an overview of Task Parallel Library (TPL) and discusses tasks. These are the foundation for the next chapters.

- Chapter 2 discusses the creation and execution of tasks. Once you execute a task, most probably, you'd like to see the result of the execution. It means that you need to wait for the task to finish its execution. Implementing a correct waiting mechanism in a multithreaded environment is extremely important. This chapter discusses different types of waiting mechanisms as well.

- Chapter 3 talks about task continuation scenarios. It also discusses nested tasks.

- Exception handling is an essential part of programming. Chapter 4 covers this topic and shows you different ways of exception handling mechanisms in task programming.

- Normally, we do not like to wait for long-running tasks. Also, if you identify a mistake early, you may not continue running the tasks. So, task cancellations are also common when you play with tasks. Chapter 5 covers this topic.

- In Chapter 6, you'll find some extra materials that were not discussed in the previous chapters.

- You can enjoy learning when you analyze case studies, ask questions (about the doubts), and do some exercises. So, throughout this book, you will see interesting program segments, "Q&A Sessions", and exercises. By analyzing these Q&As and doing the exercises, you can verify your progress. As said before, these are presented to make your future learning easier and enjoyable, but most importantly, they make you confident as a developer.

- Each question in these Q&A sessions is marked with **<chapter_no>.<Question_no>**. For example, Q2.1 means question number 1 from Chapter 2. At the end of the chapter, you'll see some exercises. You can use them to evaluate your progress. Each question in these exercises is marked with **E<chapter_no>.<Question_no>**. For example, E5.3 means exercise number 3 from Chapter 5.

- You can download all the source codes of the book from the publisher's website (`https://github.com/Apress/Task-Programming-in-C-and-.NET`).

Prerequisite Knowledge

I expect you to be very much familiar with C#. In fact, knowing about some of the advanced concepts like delegates and lambda expressions can accelerate your learning. I assume that you know how to compile or run a C# application in Visual Studio. This book does not invest time in easily available topics, such as how to install Visual Studio on your system or how to write a "Hello World" program in C#. In short, the target readers of this book are those who want to make the most out of C# by harnessing the power of both object-oriented programming (OOP) and functional programming (FP).

Who This Book Is For

You can pick the book if the answer is "yes" to the following questions:

- Are you familiar with .NET, C#, and basic object-oriented concepts like polymorphism, inheritance, abstraction, and encapsulation?

- Are you familiar with some of the advanced concepts in C# such as delegates, lambda expressions, and generics?

- Do you know how to set up your coding environment?

- Are you interested to know how the modern-day constructs of C# can help you in asynchronous and parallel programming?

Probably you shouldn't pick this book if the answer is "yes" to any of the following questions:

- Are you looking for a C# tutorial or reference book?

- Are you not ready to experiment with asynchronous programming using C# and .NET?

- "I do not like Windows, Visual Studio, and/or .NET. I want to learn asynchronous and parallel programming without them." Is this statement true for you?

Useful Software

These are the important software/tools that I used for this book:

- All the programs were tested with C# 13 and .NET 9. In this context, it is useful to know that nowadays the C# language version is automatically selected based on your project's target framework(s) so that you can always get the highest compatible version by default. In the latest versions, Visual Studio doesn't support the UI to change the value, but you can change it by editing the `csproj` file. If you are interested more in the C# language versioning, you can follow the link `https://docs.microsoft.com/en-us/dotnet/csharp/language-reference/configure-language-version`.

- During the development of this book, software updates kept coming, and I also kept updating. When I finished my initial draft, I had the latest edition of Microsoft Visual Studio Community 2022 (64-bit) – Preview Version 17.12.0 Preview 3.0. When I submitted the final draft, I had Microsoft Visual Studio Community 2022 (64-bit)-17.12.4.

- The good news for you is that this community edition is free of cost. If you do not use the Windows operating system, you can also use Visual Studio Code which is also a source code editor developed by Microsoft that runs on Windows or macOS and Linux operating systems. This multiplatform IDE is also free. However, I recommend that you check the license and privacy statement as well. It is because this statement may change in the future.

Author's note: I have tested my code only on Visual Studio. You may note that "Visual Studio 2022 for Mac" was already scheduled for retirement by August 31, 2024. To know more on this, you can refer to the online link `https://learn.microsoft.com/en-us/visualstudio/mac/what-happened-to-vs-for-mac?view=vsmac-2022`.

Guidelines for Using This Book

Here are some suggestions so that you can get the most out of this book:

- This book suits you best if you are familiar with some advanced features in C# such as delegates and lambda expressions. If not, please read those topics before you start reading this book.

- I believe that sequential reading of these chapters can help you learn faster. So, I suggest you go through the chapters sequentially. Another reason for this suggestion is that some useful and related topics may have already been discussed in a previous chapter, and I have not repeated those discussions in the later chapters.

- The programs in this book should give you the expected output in the upcoming versions of C#/Visual Studio as well. Though I believe that these results should not vary in other environments, you know the nature of software: it is naughty. So, I recommend that if you want to see the same output, it will be better if you can mimic the same environment.

- You can download and install the Visual Studio IDE from `https://visualstudio.microsoft.com/downloads/`. And you are expected to get Figure 1.

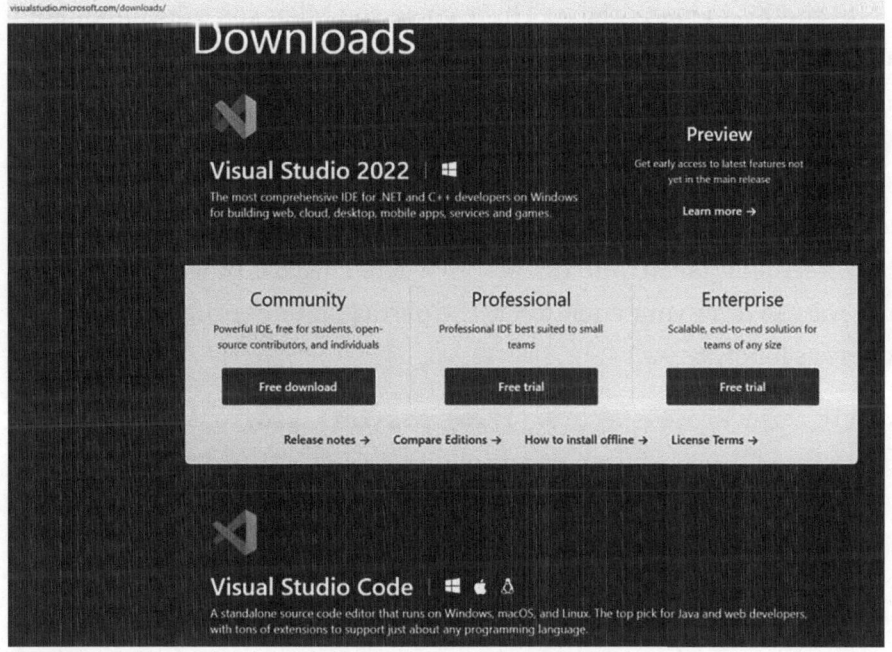

Figure 1. *The download link for Visual Studio 2022 and Visual Studio Code*

Note At the time of this writing, this link works fine, and the information is correct. However, the link and policies may change in the future. The same comment applies to all the mentioned links in this book.

Conventions Used in This Book

Here, I mention only a few points: In some places, to avoid more typing, I have used only the pronoun "he" to refer to a person when the context is generic, for example, a customer, an executive, etc. Please treat it as "he" or "she", whichever applies to you.

Secondly, in many places, I have given you Microsoft's documentation links. Why? For me, as the creators, they are the authenticated source of information to describe a feature.

Finally, all the programs, corresponding outputs, and important notes of the book follow the same font and structure. To draw your attention, in some places, I have made them bold. For example, consider the following code fragment (taken from Chapter 6) where I discuss progress reporting and want to draw your attention to the particular lines using the bold letters as follows:

```
static void ProcessRecords(IProgress<int> progress)
{
    WriteLine($"Starts processing the records...");
    int progressPercentage = 0;
    for (int i = 1; i <=5; i++)
    {
        // Varying the delay
        Thread.Sleep(i * 300);
        progressPercentage += 20;
        progress.Report(progressPercentage);
    }
    WriteLine("All the records are processed.");

}
```

Sometimes, I needed to prefix some spaces at the beginning of a few lines. It was required to indicate that you are reading a continuation of the previous line (since 'the line of code' was long, it couldn't be placed in a single line). Here is a sample (taken from Chapter 6):

```
Action greet = new(() => WriteLine($"Task {Task.CurrentId}
    says: Hello reader!"));
```

Final Words

You are an intelligent person. You have chosen a topic that can assist you throughout your career. As you learn and review these concepts, I suggest you write your code; only then will you master this area. There is no shortcut for this. Do you know the ancient story of Euclid and Ptolemy, ruler of Egypt? Euclid's approach to mathematics was based on logical reasoning and rigorous proofs, and Ptolemy asked Euclid if there was an easier way to learn mathematics. Euclid's reply to the ruler? **"There is no royal road to geometry."**

Though you are not studying geometry, the essence of this reply applies here. You must study these concepts and code. Do not give up when you face challenges. They are the indicators that you are growing better.

Errata: I have tried my level best to ensure the accuracy of the content. However, mistakes can happen. So, I have a plan to maintain the "Errata," and if required, I can also make some updates/announcements there. So, I suggest that you visit those pages to receive any important corrections or updates.

An Appeal: You can easily understand that any good quality work takes many days and many months (even years!). Many authors like me invest most of their time in writing and heavily depend on it. You can encourage and help these authors by preventing piracy. If you come across any illegal copies of our works in any form on the Internet, I would be grateful if you would provide me/the Apress team with the location address or website name. In this context, you can use the link https://www.apress.com/gp/services/rights-permission/piracy as well.

Share Your Feedback: I believe that the book is designed for you in such a way that upon its completion, you will develop an adequate knowledge of parallel programming using C# and .NET. So, I hope that you will value the effort. Once you finish reading this book, I request you to provide your valuable feedback on the Amazon review page or any other platform you like.

CHAPTER 1

Asynchronous Programming and Tasks

Starting with an introduction to asynchronous programming, this chapter quickly covers tasks and their importance.

Understanding Asynchronous Operations

Psychologists often vote for one task at a time. This is recommended for focused concentration. However, modern-day life is full of work. In our busy world, it is tough to follow this advice. For example, consider those working mothers who need to complete lots of work before they go to the office. They start preparing breakfast, and then, they come back from the kitchen to prepare the kids for school. They again go back to the kitchen to check the status and again come out from the kitchen to prepare themselves for the office. You can see that in this approach, they start a task but do not wait for that task to complete; instead, they start a new task and again go back to check the status of the old task. The process continues until all these tasks are finished. These working mothers perform the activities asynchronously.

© Vaskaran Sarcar 2025
V. Sarcar, *Task Programming in C# and .NET*, Apress Pocket Guides,
https://doi.org/10.1007/979-8-8688-1279-8_1

How Does It Help?

Even if you do not like this approach, there are situations when you cannot avoid this. For example, if you wake up late in the morning but do not want to be late for the office or school, probably you have only one option: doing tasks asynchronously.

Let us talk about programming. Suppose you develop an application where you use the main application thread to perform all kinds of work including executing long-running tasks (e.g., downloading a big file from the Internet). Since the main thread is busy while processing a long-running task, the user cannot supply any new input to the application. As a result, the application may appear blocked or frozen. From a user perspective, it is a frustrating experience.

You can make the user happy by offloading the long-running task to a background thread and making the main application thread available to do any other task. As a result, the main application thread can respond to a new user input, or it can resume the task that it was doing before invoking the long-running task. **In this way, asynchronous programming helps you develop a highly responsive application.**

You may also note that modern-day computers have multiple CPU processing cores. Using the full potential of these computers with asynchronous programming, you can make your application truly fast, efficient, and user-friendly.

Useful Scenarios

Every scenario is not suitable for asynchronous programming. For example, if the kids are naughty, probably, a mother cannot do things asynchronously. In this case, she may decide to first complete the homework before she enters the kitchen (or vice versa). This means that she needs to opt for synchronous executions only.

You may argue by saying that to reduce the work pressure, the working mother can appoint a tutor to teach her kids or a cook to prepare breakfast or meals. If this is the case, let me tell you that in such cases, she needs to increase her expenses as well. However, if there is a budget constraint, she may need to do all the work by herself. So, you can see that every scenario is not suitable for asynchronous executions (or parallel operations).

Now the question is: when should you exercise asynchronous programming? Here are some typical scenarios in which you can benefit from asynchronous programming:

- To fulfill the **I/O bound needs** such as accessing a database, reading or writing to a large file, and requesting data through the Internet

- To fulfill the **CPU-bound needs** such as performing a complex and time-consuming calculation

Q&A Session

Q1.1 It appears to me that asynchronous programming can increase the code complexity. Is this not a problem?

True. However, consider the case in which to make a more responsive UI, you offload a long-running operation to a background thread. As a result, you do not need to block the main UI thread to avoid frustrating user experience. This is appreciable because, in the end, you are making the users happy.

Q1.2 Are asynchronous and parallel programming the same?

Let us first consider some real-world examples. Suppose, you start preparing rice for dinner. Typically, after cleaning the rice, you add water and start boiling the combination over low-medium heat. Now, you need to wait until the water is absorbed. In between, you decide to give some tasks to your kids. So, you come back from the kitchen and instruct your kids to do their homework. **This is similar to asynchronous**

programming because you can go back to the kitchen and again come back to your kids until you complete these works. However, it is not equivalent to parallel programming.

Now, consider a situation when you appoint a cook to make the dinner for your family. In this case, the cook can prepare the rice, and you can focus on your kid's homework at the same time. In this case, two different people are doing two different tasks at the same time. **This is equivalent to parallel programming** with a dual-core machine.

You understand that by combining these models, you can reap benefits. For example, multiple people can be engaged in preparing the meal (consider a cook with a helper), and multiple people can teach your kids (each tutor can focus on one kid). We try to do this exactly in programming. However, the terms asynchronous programming and parallel programming are pretty close and related to each other. The *Visual Studio Magazine* summarized this by saying (see https://visualstudiomagazine.com/articles/2011/03/24/wccsp_ asynchronous-programming.aspx):

> *Asynchronous programming is a means of parallel programming in which a unit of work runs separately from the main application thread and notifies the calling thread of its completion, failure or progress.*

Programming Patterns

Undoubtedly, asynchronous programming is hard, but in earlier days, it was harder. In those days, developers had the following options:

- Direct use of threads
- Direct use of ThreadPool class
- Use of callback methods

- Use of event-based asynchrony

- Use of `AsyncResult` pattern

However, these are not recommended for the new developments.

Recommended Pattern

Then, what is the recommended pattern? See the official link `https://learn.microsoft.com/en-us/dotnet/standard/asynchronous-programming-patterns/task-based-asynchronous-pattern-tap` that states the following:

> *In .NET, the* ***task-based asynchronous pattern*** *is the recommended asynchronous design pattern for new development. It is based on the Task and Task<TResult> types in the System.Threading.Tasks namespace, which are used to represent asynchronous operations.*

However, this book does not discuss task-based asynchronous pattern (TAP) in detail. This is because most of the TAP implementations involve the `async` and `await` keywords which will be discussed in another pocketbook in this learning series. This book is purely focused on task programming without using them. Understanding these topics will immensely help when you deep dive into asynchronous programming and start applying `async` and `await` in your programs.

Task Parallel Library (TPL)

In task programming, you'll often hear about the task parallel library (TPL). Let me give you a quick overview of that. TPL provides a set of public types and APIs which are available in the following namespaces:

- System.Threading

- System.Threading.Tasks

You may note that the System.Threading.Tasks namespace was introduced in .NET 4 and Microsoft stated (see https://learn. microsoft.com/en-us/dotnet/standard/parallel-programming/task-parallel-library-tpl) the following:

TPL is the preferred API for writing multi-threaded, asynchronous, and parallel code in .NET

This is why this book starts the discussion with tasks that are the foundation of the Task Parallel Library (TPL).

Note   It is interesting to know that behind the scenes, tasks are queued to the ThreadPool that determines and adjusts the number of threads. The ThreadPool follows some algorithms to control the load balancing to gain maximum throughput.

How Does TPL Help?

TPL is useful in many different scenarios. For example, you can use TPL to control any of the following scenarios:

- Managing a multithreaded environment efficiently
- Scaling the concurrency level
- Providing support for task cancellations
- State management
- Partitioning your work

For now, it will be sufficient for you to understand that TPL simplifies the multithread scenarios and helps you write high-performance code without worrying about the nitty-gritty of threading or other low-level details. The following statement from Microsoft (see https://learn.

microsoft.com/en-us/dotnet/standard/parallel-programming/task-parallel-library-tpl) nicely summarizes the usefulness of TPL:

The purpose of the TPL is to make developers more productive by simplifying the process of adding parallelism and concurrency to applications.

Introducing Tasks

TPL is based on the concept of tasks. So, the question is: what is a task? You can consider a task as a code block that represents a unit of work. You can inform the scheduler that this code block can execute on a separate thread while the main thread can continue its execution. For example, consider the following code segment:

```
static void PrintNumbersTask()
{
    WriteLine("Starts printing the numbers.");
    // Continues the work
    WriteLine("The task is completed.");
}
```

This can be a unit of work that can be executed on a separate thread.

Useful Scenarios

The following list includes some common scenarios where you can use tasks:

- Performing a calculation and displaying the result

- Computing a value with/without a supplied input

- Asking for a network resource

- Checking the health of a website, for example, pinging a website

Q&A Session

Q1.3 What are the benefits of using tasks over threads?

Here are some common benefits:

- The tasks are relatively lightweight. They help you achieve **fine-grained parallelism.**

- Later, you'll see that by using the in-built API for tasks, you easily exercise useful operations such as waiting, cancellations, continuations, custom scheduling, or robust exception handling. So, when you opt for tasks instead of threads, you'll have **more programmatic control.**

Q1.4 What were the fundamental advances in task over the previous programming models?

There are many benefits. Once you complete this book, these benefits will be apparent to you. For now, you may note that while using tasks, after you initiate the operation(s), you can easily connect the producer of the task and consumer(s) of the task by providing a continuation of work. More specifically, you do not need to provide the continuation work to the method that invokes the operation. It is one of the primary benefits of using tasks over the previous programming models.

Summary

This chapter started with a discussion on asynchronous programming and its usage in the current world. Then, it introduced TPL and the role of tasks in asynchronous programming. In brief, it answered the following questions:

- What is asynchronous programming and why is it important?

- What are the ideal scenarios for asynchronous programming?

- What is TPL?

- What is a task and why is it beneficial over threads?

Exercises

Check your understanding by attempting the following exercises:

E1.1 State True/False:

i)   In .NET, the task-based asynchronous pattern is the current recommended pattern for asynchronous programming.

ii) Asynchronous executions are always faster than the corresponding synchronous executions.

iii) Performing a time-consuming computation is an example of CPU-bound operation that can benefit from asynchronous programming.

iv) Downloading a large file from the Internet is a common example of an I/O-bound operation that can benefit from asynchronous programming.

E1.2 Can you mention at least two primary benefits of exercising asynchronous programming?

Solutions to Exercises

Here is a sample solution set for the exercises in this chapter.

E1.1

The answers are shown inline in bold:

i)   In .NET, the task-based asynchronous pattern is the current recommended pattern for asynchronous programming. [**True**]

ii) Asynchronous executions are always faster than the corresponding synchronous executions. [**False**]

iii) Performing a time-consuming computation is an example of CPU-bound operation that can benefit from asynchronous programming. [**True**]

iv) Downloading a large file from the Internet is a common example of an I/O-bound operation that can benefit from asynchronous programming. [**True**]

E1.2

The following list includes two primary benefits of using an asynchronous application:

- You can offload the long-running tasks to the background threads. As a result, you can build more responsive user interfaces.

- Using asynchronous programming, you can take full advantage of modern-day hardware to speed up your application.

CHAPTER 2

Task Creation and Execution

This chapter helps you dive into task programming. Here, you'll learn different ways to create and execute tasks. Once you execute a task, you may be interested to see the result. It means that you need to wait for the task completion. This is why this chapter discusses different kinds of waiting mechanisms as well.

Creating and Executing a Task

You can create and execute tasks in different ways. Suppose you have the following code:

```
static void DoSomeTask()
{
    // Some code
}
```

Given the following code, let me show you the common approaches for task creation and execution:

© Vaskaran Sarcar 2025
V. Sarcar, *Task Programming in C# and .NET*, Apress Pocket Guides,
https://doi.org/10.1007/979-8-8688-1279-8_2

Approach-1:

The Task.Run method is the recommended and most common to create and start a task. This approach helps you automatically start the task after creation. Here is a sample code:

```
Task task = Task.Run(DoSomeTask);
```

Approach-2:

To create a task and automatically start the execution, you can use the Task.Factory.StartNew method as well. Using this approach, you can exercise advanced options to configure tasks. Here is a sample code:

```
Task task = Task.Factory.StartNew(DoSomeTask);
```

Approach-3:

In addition, you can use the Task constructor to create a task. However, in this case, you need to explicitly start it by calling the Start method. Here is a sample code:

```
Task task = new Task(DoSomeTask);
task.Start();
```

C# 9 onward, you can use target-typed new expressions. So, the previous code block can be further simplified as follows:

```
Task task = new(DoSomeTask);
task.Start();
```

Note   You have seen the approaches that **explicitly** create and execute tasks. There are other approaches as well. For example, you can **implicitly** create and execute tasks using **Parallel.Invoke** method. In addition, **TaskCompletionSource<TResult>** class also helps you create specialized tasks that are suitable for particular scenarios. However, let us learn the concepts one at a time.

Encapsulating Code Using Lambda Expression

You can create a task by providing a delegate that encapsulates the intended code. This delegate can be expressed as a named delegate, an anonymous method, or a lambda expression. This is why I present you another task example, where I encapsulate the necessary code inside a lambda expression as follows:

```
Task task = Task.Run(
    () =>
    {
        // Some code to execute
    }
);
```

Demonstration 1

Let us verify whether tasks help us perform asynchronous programming using the following demonstration:

POINT TO REMEMBER

.NET 6 onward, you may notice the presence of implicit global directives for new C# projects. This helps you use the types in these namespaces without specifying the fully qualified names or manually adding a "using directive." You can learn more about this from the online link https://learn.microsoft. com/en-us/dotnet/core/project-sdk/overview#implicit-using-directives.

For the C# projects in this book, I did not change the default settings. As a result, you will not see me mentioning the following namespaces that were available by default:

System
System.Collections.Generic
System.IO
System.Linq
System.Net.Http
System.Threading
System.Threading.Tasks

```csharp
using static System.Console;

WriteLine("The main thread starts executing.");

Task.Run(PrintNumbers);

WriteLine($"The main thread is doing some other work...");
// Simulating a delay
Thread.Sleep(10);

WriteLine($"The main thread is completed.");
ReadKey();

static void PrintNumbers()
{
    for (int i = 1; i <= 5; i++)
    {
        Write($" {i}\t");
        // Simulating a delay
        Thread.Sleep(2);
    }
}
```

Output

Here is a sample output of this program from my computer. It is obvious that the output can vary in your system. You can see that the main thread was not blocked during the execution of the printing task. There is a nice mixture of output from all the different threads/tasks.

```
The main thread starts executing.
The main thread is doing some other work...
 1       2       3       The main thread is completed.
 4       5
```

Q&A Session

Q2.1 To create and execute tasks you have shown me the use of Run, Start, and StartNew methods. How can I decide which one is best for me?

If you see the method definitions in Visual Studio, you will see the following statement: "The **Start** method starts the System.Threading. Tasks.Task, scheduling it for execution to the specified System. Threading.Tasks.TaskScheduler." This method is useful when you manually execute the task depending on some condition.

The **Run** method queues the specified work to run on the thread pool and returns a System.Threading.Tasks.Task object that represents that work. This is a lightweight alternative to the StartNew method. It helps you start a task with the default values. This indicates that the **Run** method uses the default task scheduler, regardless of a task scheduler that is associated with the current thread. This is why Microsoft (see https://learn. microsoft.com/en-us/dotnet/standard/parallel-programming/task-based-asynchronous-programming) provides the following suggestions:

- The Run methods are the preferred way to create and start tasks when more control over the creation and scheduling of the task isn't needed.

Microsoft further says (see the same link) that you can use the StartNew method for the following situations (see the same link):

- Creation and scheduling don't have to be separated, and you require additional task creation options or the use of a specific scheduler.

- You need to pass an additional state into the task that you can retrieve through its Task.AsyncState property.

POINT TO NOTE

To give you a specific example, let me tell you that you'll learn about child tasks (or nested tasks) shortly. There you'll see that using TaskCreationOptions.AttachedToParent, you can attach a child task to the parent task (if the parent task allows this activity). This option is available in some of the overloads of the StartNew method. However, the Run method does not provide a similar option.

Passing and Returning Values

In this section, I'll discuss how you can pass value(s) to a task or get back a computed value from a task.

Passing Values into Tasks

In Demonstration 1, the PrintNumber method printed the numbers from 1 to 5. Let us modify this function, so that it can accept arguments. Here is the modified function with the key changes in bold:

```
static void PrintNumbers(int limit)
{
    for (int i = 1; i <= limit; i++)
    {
        Write($" {i}\t");
        // Simulating a delay
        Thread.Sleep(2);
    }
}
```

If you want to execute this function on a separate thread, you need to pass a valid argument (for the limit parameter) from the calling thread. So, let us change the following line of Demonstration 1:

```
Task task = Task.Run(PrintNumbers);
```

with the following one:

```
Task task = Task.Run(()=>PrintNumbers(5));
```

Now, if you run the program again, you'll see the similar output that you already saw by running Demonstration 1.

I assume that I do not need to remind you that you can replace the previous line of code with the following line:

```
Task task = Task.Factory.StartNew(() => PrintNumbers(5));
```

Or the following lines:

```
Task task = new (() => PrintNumbers(5));
task.Start();
```

Let us investigate an alternative approach. At the time of this writing, the Task class has the following constructors (see Figure 2-1).

```
...public class Task : IAsyncResult, IDisposable
{
    ...public Task(Action action);
    ...public Task(Action action, CancellationToken cancellationToken);
    ...public Task(Action action, TaskCreationOptions creationOptions);
    ...public Task(Action<object?> action, object? state);
    ...public Task(Action action, CancellationToken cancellationToken, TaskCreationOptions creationOptions);
    ...public Task(Action<object?> action, object? state, CancellationToken cancellationToken);
    ...public Task(Action<object?> action, object? state, TaskCreationOptions creationOptions);
    ...public Task(Action<object?> action, object? state, CancellationToken cancellationToken, TaskCreationOpt
```

Figure 2-1. *The partial snapshot shows the overloaded versions of the Task constructors*

Notice the following constructor that is already highlighted in Figure 2-1:

```
public Task(Action<object?> action, object? state);
```

This constructor gives you the idea that you can pass an `object` argument to them. So, let me introduce another function called `PrintNumbersVersion2` that takes an `object` parameter and does a similar thing. It is as follows (notice the changes in bold):

```
static void PrintNumbersVersion2(object? state)
{
    int limit = Convert.ToInt32(state);
    for (int i = 0; i <= limit; i++)
    {
        Write($" {i}\t");
        // Doing remaining things, if any
        Thread.Sleep(2);
    }
}
```

This time, you can write something like

```
Task task = new(PrintNumbersVersion2, 5);
task.Start();
```

Or

```
Task task = Task.Factory.StartNew(PrintNumbersVersion2, 5);
```

However, the Run method does not have any such constructor. So, you cannot write something like

```
Task task4 = Task.Run(PrintNumbersVersion2, 5); // Error
```

Ok, you have already seen many different approaches while passing a state so far. Let us summarize them:

```
// Approach-1:
var task1 = Task.Run(() => PrintNumbers(10));

// Approach-2:
var task2=Task.Factory.StartNew(() => PrintNumbers(10));

// Approach-3:
var task3 = new Task(() => PrintNumbers(10));
task3.Start();

// Approach-4:
var task4 = new Task(PrintNumbersVersion2,10);
task4.Start();

// Approach-5:
var task5 = Task.Factory.StartNew(PrintNumbersVersion2,10);
```

You can see that in each approach, I passed an int. However, in the last two cases, the target method (PrintNumbersVersion2) expected an object. As a result, these two approaches suffer from the impact of boxing and unboxing. On the contrary, they look cleaner compared to approaches 1, 2, or 3. In the end, it is up to you how you want to organize it.

Note   Download the project **Chapter2_Demo2A_PassingValues** to experience the different approaches that you have seen till now.

Returning Values from Tasks

When you execute a task, you may need to access the final value. In such cases, you need to use the generic version of the Task class and the Result property. Here is a sample:

```
var task = Task<string>.Run(() => "Hello");
var result = task.Result;
WriteLine(result);
```

However, the type argument can be inferred, and as a result, you can further simplify this code as follows:

```
var task = Task.Run(() => "Hello");
var result = task.Result;
WriteLine(result);
```

POINT TO NOTE

In the previous code segments, I have used the var type to type less. Here is an equivalent code that explicitly shows the types:

```
Task<string> task = Task.Run(() => "Hello");
string result = task.Result;
WriteLine(result);
```

Demonstration 2

Let us see a complete program that deals with some tasks, passes some values into them, and finally, retrieves the computed result.

In the following demonstration, I create a task that adds two integers (10 and 20). Once the task is completed, I retrieve the computed result and display it in the console window. Let us see the complete program now:

```
using static System.Console;

static int Add(int number1, int number2) => number1 + number2;

WriteLine("Passing and returning values by executing tasks.");
int firstNumber = 10;
int SecondNumber = 20;

var addTask = Task.Run(() => Add(firstNumber, SecondNumber));
var result = addTask.Result;

WriteLine($"{firstNumber}+{SecondNumber}={result}");
WriteLine($"The main thread is completed.");
```

Output

Here is the output:

```
Passing and returning values by executing tasks.
10+20=30
The main thread is completed.
```

Q&A Session

Q2.2 I can see that in the previous demonstration, you did not use the ReadKey method to prevent the end of the console mode application. Was it intentional?

When you want to get a result from a task, you need to wait until the task finishes its execution. It means that you need to invoke a blocking operation. Using the Result property, I did the same: I blocked the calling thread until the invoked task finished its execution. As a result, I did not need to use any more blocking constructs.

Author's note: Task instances can use the Wait method as well for a task to complete execution. Shortly, you'll see a discussion on different kinds of waiting mechanisms.

Understanding the Problem in Demonstration 2

Notice that in the previous output, the line "The main thread is completed." appeared at the end of the output. If you execute the program several times, you'll always notice the same. It is because by calling the Result method, I forced the main thread to wait for the addTask to complete. As a result, we could not take full advantage of asynchronous programming. The same problem occurs if you use the Wait method as well.

Q&A Session

Q2.3 I understand that using the blocking calls like var result = addTask. Result; or addTask.Wait(); you effectively make the code synchronous. Then, why did you show me the program that uses the blocking calls?

I wanted you to be aware of it. In addition, there will be situations where you cannot proceed until you get a result from an intended task. In those cases, you cannot avoid blocking calls (Demonstration 3 will give you an idea about this). So, if you consider using it, try to do so after running other code that can run asynchronously. However, do not worry! Shortly, you'll see the discussion on nonblocking calls as well.

Discussion on Waiting

There are different built-in constructs for waiting. In this section, let me show you the need for "waiting" and discuss some useful methods to implement the idea.

Note   To get a result of a task execution, if you block the calling thread, you are not taking advantage of asynchronous programming. So, it is important to design your application accordingly.

Why Do We Wait?

Once you execute a task, you may like to get the result. It means that you need to wait for the task to finish its execution. The following demonstration gives you the idea.

Demonstration 3

In the following program, the calling thread (aka main thread) invokes two different tasks. Let us execute the program and analyze some of the possible outputs:

```
using static System.Console;

WriteLine("The main thread starts.");

var printLuckyNumberTask = Task.Run(
    () =>
```

```
    {
        WriteLine("Wait for your lucky number...");
        // Simulating a delay
        Thread.Sleep(1);
        WriteLine($"---Your lucky number is: {new Random().
        Next(1,10)}");
    }
);

var processOrderTask = Task.Run(
    () =>
    {
        WriteLine("Processing an order...");
        // Simulating a delay
        Thread.Sleep(200);
        WriteLine($"---Your order is processed.");
    }
);
WriteLine("The end of main.");
```

Output

Here I include some possible outputs from my computer:

Output 1:

```
The main thread starts.
The end of main.
```

Output 2:

```
The main thread starts.
The end of main.
Processing an order...
Wait for your lucky number...
```

Analysis

These outputs reflect the following characteristics:

- The main thread ends before `printLuckyNumberTask` and `processOrderTask` finish their executions.

- None of these outputs reflect whether the invoked tasks complete their job.

How Do We Wait?

You understand that to see the final status of these tasks, you may need to wait for some more time. How can you wait? There are different approaches. Let me show you some of them in the following section.

Using Sleep

Probably, one of the simplest solutions is to block the main thread until other tasks are finished. Here is a sample where I block the main thread for 1000 milliseconds:

```
// The previous code is the same
Thread.Sleep(1000);
WriteLine("The end of main.");
```

Note   You can download the project Chapter2_DiscussionOnWaiting from the Apress website to run and validate all the program segments that are discussed in this section.

27

This one line of additional code increases the probability of seeing an output that reflects these two tasks completing their executions before the control leaves the main thread. Here is a possible output:

```
The main thread starts.
Processing an order...
Wait for your lucky number...
---Your lucky number is: 3
---Your order is processed.
The end of main.
```

The advantage of using this approach is obvious. We can see that when the main thread sleeps, other tasks could execute their job. It indicates that during sleep, the scheduler can schedule other tasks.

On the contrary, this approach has an obvious problem: you may block the thread unnecessarily for some additional time. For example, I can see a similar output (I am saying "similar" instead of "same" because the generated random number keeps varying which is an expected behavior for this program) in my computer if I block the main thread for 500 milliseconds or less too. **However, the problem is that since we cannot predict the exact time for these tasks to be completed, I need to block it for a reasonable amount of time.** So, if any of these tasks take more time to complete due to some other factors, you may not see the task's completion message in the output. This is a problem for sure!

Neither we want unnecessary waiting nor do we want to miss any key information. From this point of view, it is an inefficient approach. In fact, the situation can be worse if you work on an application that tries to block the UI. This is why relying on the Sleep method may not always be a good idea.

Using Delay

In the previous code, let me replace the statement, Thread.Sleep(1000); with Task.Delay(1000); in the main thread as follows:

```
// The previous code is the same
Task.Delay(1000);
WriteLine("The end of main.");
```

and run the program again. Again, my computer shows different possible outputs, and one of them is as follows:

```
The main thread starts.
Processing an order...
The end of main.
Wait for your lucky number...
```

This output reflects that the calling thread was not blocked for the printLuckyNumberTask and processOrderTask to complete their job. So, you see the line "The end of main." before the order was processed or the lucky number was displayed. **This gives you a clue that you should use Sleep for the synchronous pauses, whereas you should prefer the Delay method for nonblocking delays. This is why the use of the Delay method can help you build a more responsive UI.**

In fact, Visual Studio IDE will give you a clue about this. Let me explain this: Once you learn more about asynchronous programming, you'll know that the use of async and await keywords simplifies asynchronous programming. Then, you may write something like the following: await Task.Delay(1000);. However, without using the await keyword, if you use the line Task.Delay(1000); you'll see the following warning message:

> *CS4014 Because this call is not awaited, execution of the current method continues before the call is completed. Consider applying the 'await' operator to the result of the call.*

MORE ON SLEEP VS. DELAY

While using the Delay method, you can also assign it to a task and "await" at a later point in time as follows:

```
Task task= Task.Delay(1000);
// Do something here
await task;
```

In addition, the Delay method has various overloads, and many of them accept CancellationToken as a parameter (this is discussed in the next chapter). Using this parameter, you can avoid aborting the thread and terminate it nicely.

Using ReadKey() or ReadLine()

Sometimes, you see the presence of ReadKey(), Read(), or ReadLine() in a program. The basic idea of using these methods is to block the control of execution until the user provides the required input. For example, you can wait for printLuckyNumberTask and processOrderTask to finish their executions, and then, you can press a key from the keyboard to get the final output. Here is a sample code:

```
// The previous code is the same
ReadKey();
WriteLine("The end of main");
```

Using Wait

Demonstration 2 showed that by using the Result property, you can block the calling thread until the specific task is finished. However, it is not necessary that in every scenario, you analyze the outcome of task execution. In fact, a task may not return a value as well. So, let me show you another waiting technique.

Invoking the Wait method on a Task instance, you can wait for it to complete. Here is a sample where I call Wait on printLuckyNumberTask and processOrderTask separately:

```
// The previous code is the same
printLuckyNumberTask.Wait();
processOrderTask.Wait();
WriteLine("The end of main.");
```

This change allows both tasks to finish their executions.

Using WaitAll

Instead of waiting for the individual tasks to be completed, you can wait for a group of tasks. In such cases, you use the WaitAll method and provide the task objects for which you want to wait as parameters. Here is a sample:

```
// The previous code is the same
Task.WaitAll(printLuckyNumberTask, processOrderTask);
WriteLine("The end of main.");
```

This change can also produce an output where you'll see that both tasks finished their executions.

Using WaitAny

Suppose there are multiple tasks, but you'd like to wait for any of them to complete. In such cases, you use the WaitAny method as follows:

```
// The previous code is the same
Task.WaitAny(printLuckyNumberTask, processOrderTask);
WriteLine("The end of main.");
```

Here is a sample output:

```
The main thread starts.
Wait for your lucky number...
Processing an order...
---Your lucky number is: 2
The end of main.
```

This output shows that this time the main thread did not wait for the processOrderTask to finish its execution.

POINTS TO NOTE

These methods have various overloads. For example, at the time of this writing, the Wait method has six different overloads. Using these overloaded versions, you can provide a maximum duration to wait, a CancellationToken instance, or both of them to monitor while waiting.

Using WhenAny

Notice the previous output once again. You can see that the line "The end of main." came after at least one of the tasks finished its execution. If you execute the program repeatedly, you'll never see that the mentioned line appears before at least one task finishes its execution. It is because, **in the case of WaitAny, the calling thread is blocked till any of those tasks finishes the execution.** Interestingly, there is another method, called WhenAny, that does not block the calling thread.

Consider the following code where I replace WaitAny with WhenAny:

```
// The previous code is the same
Task.WhenAny(printLuckyNumberTask, processOrderTask);
WriteLine("The end of main.");
```

Here is a sample output after this change:

```
The main thread starts.
The end of main.
Processing an order...
Wait for your lucky number...
```

You can see that the main thread was not blocked in this case.

Waiting For Cancellation

There will be situations when you need to be prepared for possible cancellations of tasks. In those cases, you need to have a cancellation token. Since the topic is important as well as big, I have discussed it in a separate chapter (Chapter 5).

Q&A Session

Q2.4 In some blogs/articles, I see the usage of Thread.SpinWait, instead of Thread.Sleep. How do they differ?

The SpinWait method is useful for implementing locks but not for ordinary applications. When you use spin waiting, the scheduler does not pass the control to some other task, which means it avoids context switching. The online link https://learn.microsoft.com/en-us/dotnet/api/system.threading.thread.spinwait?view=net-9.0 states:

> *In the rare case where it is advantageous to avoid a context switch, such as when you know that a state change is imminent, make a call to the SpinWait method in your loop. The code SpinWait executes is designed to prevent problems that can occur on computers with multiple processors. For example, on computers with multiple Intel processors employing Hyper-Threading technology, SpinWait prevents processor starvation in certain situations.*

Note   The .NET Framework classes such as `Monitor` or `ReaderWriterLock` internally use the `SpinWait` method. Still, instead of using this method directly, Microsoft recommends that you use the built-in synchronization classes to serve your purpose. I also recommend not using this method for one typical reason: `SpinWait` accepts an integer argument that represents the number of iterations for the CPU loop to be performed. As a result, the waiting time depends on the processor's speed.

It is useful to note that you can use the `SpinUntil` method as well. At the time of this writing, there are three overloaded versions of this method:

```
SpinUntil(Func<Boolean>)
SpinUntil(Func<Boolean>, Int32)
SpinUntil(Func<Boolean>, TimeSpan)
```

Let me show you a usage of the simplest version that spins until the specified condition is fulfilled. Here is a sample for you where I wait until `printLuckyNumberTask` completes its execution properly:

```
// Previous code is the same. You can see it by downloading
// the Chapter2_DiscussionOnWaiting project
SpinWait.SpinUntil(() =>
 printLuckyNumberTask.Status ==  TaskStatus.RanToCompletion);
WriteLine("The end of main.");
```

Here is a possible output after this change is made to this program:

```
The main thread starts.
Processing an order...
Wait for your lucky number...
---Your lucky number is: 8
The end of main.
```

Note that this time the output shows that `printLuckyNumberTask` completes the execution but it does not reflect whether `processOrderTask` completes the execution. It is because I cared about the status of the `printLuckyNumberTask` only.

POINT TO NOTE

The key takeaway is that there are different ways of waiting. You can use the one which is more convenient for you. I am mentioning only those methods that will be sufficient for you to understand the rest of this book. Remember that these methods have various overloaded versions as well.

Q2.5 Give me an example where you'd like to use WhenAny or WaitAny. Between these two methods, which one would you like to use?

Suppose you are working with two different tasks and each task works with a different URL. Let us further assume that each URL can help you test the current health of a website. You understand that any of these links will be sufficient to check the current status of a website. So, your program can execute the tasks and continue as soon as you get the data. In such a case, you can use `WhenAny` or `WaitAny`.

Unless there are sufficient reasons, I'll opt for `WhenAny` in such a case for the following reasons:

- It is nonblocking.

- The previous point is important to avoid deadlocks as well. For example, consider a situation when you deal with multiple tasks. Let's assume that the main application thread waits to get a notification from another task, say either from taskA or from taskB. However, if both tasks (taskA and taskB) stop executing due to some unpredictable circumstances, the main thread is blocked as well. In fact, the use of `WaitAny` can cause deadlock as well.

35

Summary

This chapter gave you a quick overview of task creations and executions. It also described different waiting mechanisms for task completions. In brief, it answered the following questions:

- What is a task and how can you create a task?

- How can you pass values into tasks?

- How can you return a value from a task?

- How can you employ a waiting mechanism in task programming?

Exercises

Check your understanding by attempting the following exercises:

POINT TO REMEMBER

As said before, for all code examples, the "Implicit Global Usings" was enabled in Visual Studio. This is why you'll not see me mentioning the following namespaces that were available by default:

```
System
System.Collections.Generic
System.IO
System.Linq
System.Net.Http
System.Threading
System.Threading.Tasks
```

The same comment applies to all exercises in this book as well.

E2.1 If you execute the following code, can you predict the output?

```
using static System.Console;

Task printHelloTask = new(
    () => WriteLine("Hello!")
);
printHelloTask.Wait(1);
WriteLine("End.");
```

E2.2 Can you predict the output of the following program?

```
using static System.Console;
Task welcomeTask = Task.Run(
    () =>
    {
        Thread.Sleep(5);
        WriteLine("Welcome!");
    }
);
Thread.Sleep(2);
WriteLine("How are you doing?");
```

E2.3 Can you predict the output of the following program?

```
using static System.Console;
var sayHello = (string msg = "Hello, reader!") => msg;
var displayMsgTask = Task.Run(()=>WriteLine(sayHello()));
displayMsgTask.Wait();
WriteLine("Goodbye.");
```

E2.4 Write a function that accepts a number to calculate its factorial. Execute the function with a background thread and display the result on the console. (You do not need to consider typical input validations or exceptional scenarios for this program.)

E2.5 State True/False:

i) The WaitAny method blocks the calling thread, but the WhenAny method does not block the calling thread.

ii) To build a more responsive UI, you should prefer the Sleep method over the Delay method.

Solutions to Exercises

Here is a sample solution set for the exercises in this chapter.

E2.1

Notice that you have created the task but you have not started this task. So, the program will output the following:

```
End.
```

E2.2

The program can show more than one possible output. However, notice that you did not wait for the task to finish its execution. So, depending on the computer's speed, the order of the output statements can vary. Here is one sample output:

```
How are you doing?
Welcome!
```

It is also possible that in the output, you see "How are you doing?" only if the task takes some more time to start. To examine this, you can run the following code in which by introducing some more delay inside welcomeTask (see the bold line), I increase the probability of finishing the main thread early:

```
using static System.Console;
Task welcomeTask = Task.Run(
    () =>
    {
        //Thread.Sleep(5);
        Thread.Sleep(200);
        WriteLine("Welcome!");
    }
);
Thread.Sleep(2);
WriteLine("How are you doing?");
```

E2.3

C#12 allows you to define default values for parameters on lambda expressions. So the code can be compiled without any issues. In addition, this time the output is also predictable because the main thread must wait for the task to finish. So, you will see the following output:

```
Hello, reader!
Goodbye.
```

E2.4

Here is a sample solution that calculates the factorial of 10 using a background task:

```
using static System.Console;
WriteLine("The main thread initiates the task.");
var calculateFactorialTask = Task.Run(() =>
CalculateFactorial(10));
```

```
WriteLine("The main thread resumes to do other things.");
WriteLine($"The factorial of 10 is: {calculateFactorialTask.
    Result}");

static int CalculateFactorial(int number)
{
    int temp = 1;
    for (int i = 2; i <= number; i++)
    {
        temp *= i;
    }
    return temp;
}
```

Here is the sample output for your reference:

```
The main thread initiates the task.
The main thread resumes to do other things.
The factorial of 10 is: 3628800
```

E2.5

The answers are shown inline in bold:

i)   The WaitAny method blocks the calling thread, but the WhenAny method does not block the calling thread. [**True**]

ii) To build a more responsive UI, you should prefer the Sleep method over the Delay method. [**False**]

CHAPTER 3

Continuation and Nested Tasks

This chapter will give you an overview of task continuations, nested tasks, and related topics.

Continuation Tasks

Suppose, there are two tasks, called Task A and Task B. If you want to start executing Task B only after Task A, probably you'd like to use callbacks. But TPL makes it easy. It provides the functionality through a continuation task which is nothing but an asynchronous task. The idea is the same: once an antecedent task finishes, it invokes the next task that you want to continue. **In our example, Task A is the antecedent task and Task B is the continuation task.** Let me summarize the important characteristics of a continuation task:

- A continuation task is invoked by another task. It can start when the prior task (i.e., the antecedent task) is completed. It means continuations are nothing but chaining tasks.

- Using this concept, you can pass data (as well as exceptions) from an antecedent to the continuation task.

© Vaskaran Sarcar 2025
V. Sarcar, *Task Programming in C# and .NET*, Apress Pocket Guides,
https://doi.org/10.1007/979-8-8688-1279-8_3

- If an asynchronous task returns some data, you can use the continuation to receive and/or process that data without blocking the main thread. This makes continuations very flexible.

- The continuations can be attached to one or more antecedents.

- You can invoke single as well as multiple continuation tasks.

- You can control the continuation. For example, if there are three tasks, called Task A, Task B, and Task C, you can decide that Task C should continue only after both Task A and Task B finish their executions. Alternatively, you may decide that Task C should not wait for both Task A and Task B; instead, it should continue when any of them finish the execution.

- You can also cancel a continuation task if you want. This is often useful during an emergency or when you find a typical bug that keeps occurring during the execution of an application.

Simple Continuation

Assume that a person, named Jack, wants to invite his friends to a dinner party. At a high level, let us divide the overall activity into two different tasks as follows:

- Inviting friends

- Ordering food

Let us assume that Jack first invites his friends over the phone. Once the invitation is done, he has an idea of how many people are joining the party. Based on that, now he orders the food. You can see that inviting friends is the antecedent task and ordering food is the continuation task. Let us develop a program to mimic the scenario.

For the continuation task, you'll notice the use of the ContinueWith method. This method creates a continuation that executes when the target task is completed. There are many overloads of this method. In this example, I use the simplest version of ContinueWith that accepts an Action<Task> as the parameter. This is why you will see the following code block:

```
var orderTask = inviteTask.ContinueWith(previousTask =>
    {
        WriteLine(previousTask.Result);
        // Simulating a delay to mimic a real-world situation
        Thread.Sleep(1000);
        WriteLine("Food is ordered now.");
    }
);
```

You can see that I inserted a one-second pause inside orderTask. Though it was not required, I kept this line of code to mimic the delay between the task of inviting friends and ordering food.

POINT TO NOTE

To show you the complete output, I use the ReadLine method in this example to prevent the end of the console mode application. The same comment applies whenever you see me using the ReadKey or ReadLine method in the demonstrations of this book.

Demonstration 1

Here is the complete demonstration:

```
using static System.Console;

WriteLine("The host is planning a party.");
var inviteTask = Task.Run(() => "Invitation is done.");
var orderTask = inviteTask.ContinueWith(previousTask =>
    {
        WriteLine(previousTask.Result);
        // Simulating a delay to mimic a real-world situation
        Thread.Sleep(1000);
        WriteLine("Food is ordered now.");
    }
);
WriteLine("The host is decorating the house.");
ReadLine();
```

Output

Here is a sample output for you:

```
The host is planning a party.
The host is decorating the house.
Invitation is done.
Food is ordered now.
```

Analysis

The previous output confirms the following characteristics:

- The main thread was not blocked while the continuation task was running. This is why you see the line "The host is decorating the house." before the line "Invitation is done."

- You can also see that the continuation task started after the antecedent task finished. In addition, it successfully processed the data that was returned from the parent/antecedent task.

- In this example, when the continuation task processed the line WriteLine(previousTask.Result); **it was nonblocking.** Why? Since the previous task was already completed, its result was instantly available.

Conditional Continuations

Demonstration 1 shows you a simple continuation example. However, you can have more control over the continuation process. Let us examine this concept with some case studies.

Case Study 1

Even after inviting the guests, the host may need to shift the party due to some unavoidable circumstances. In this case, instead of ordering the food, let us assume that the host lets the guest know about the situation and shifts the party date. Can you write a program to mimic the situation?

Surely, you can. However, let me show a technique that manages the situation using the TaskContinuationOptions enumeration. The following screenshot (see Figure 3-1) from Visual Studio shows you the different members of TaskContinuationOptions:

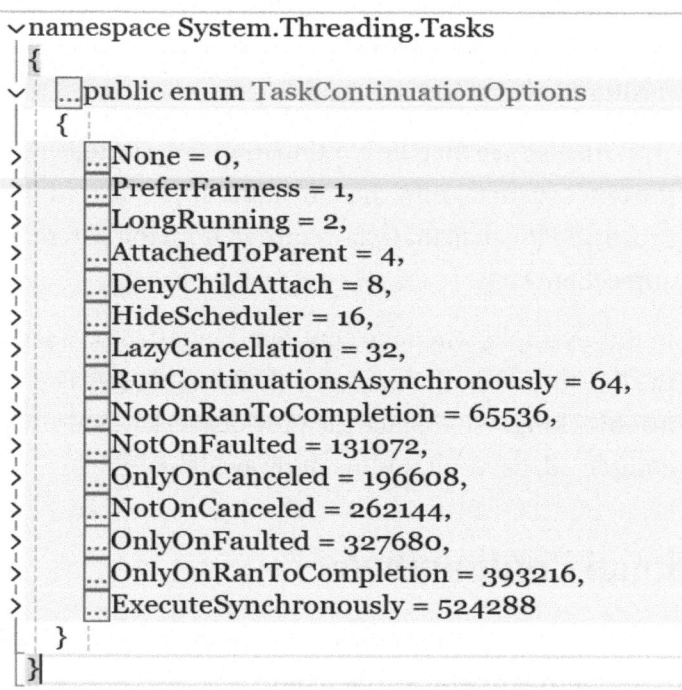

```
namespace System.Threading.Tasks
{
    public enum TaskContinuationOptions
    {
        None = 0,
        PreferFairness = 1,
        LongRunning = 2,
        AttachedToParent = 4,
        DenyChildAttach = 8,
        HideScheduler = 16,
        LazyCancellation = 32,
        RunContinuationsAsynchronously = 64,
        NotOnRanToCompletion = 65536,
        NotOnFaulted = 131072,
        OnlyOnCanceled = 196608,
        NotOnCanceled = 262144,
        OnlyOnFaulted = 327680,
        OnlyOnRanToCompletion = 393216,
        ExecuteSynchronously = 524288
    }
}
```

Figure 3-1. *The members of TaskContinuationOptions*

Note   Discussing all these members will make the book unnecessarily fat. If interested, you can learn more about these members by expanding them in Visual Studio or from the online link https://learn.microsoft.com/en-us/dotnet/api/ system.threading.tasks.taskcontinuationoptions?vi ew=net-8.0. However, I believe that you can get some idea about these members by seeing their names as well.

Since our example deals with an exceptional situation, I am going to use NotOnFaulted and OnlyOnFaulted options. You can safely assume that the NotOnFaulted option will be used for the normal situation and the other one will be used to deal with an exceptional situation.

Before you see the complete program, let me tell you that to generate an exceptional situation, I have used a dummy logic. It is as follows: *The antecedent task (**inviteTask**) generates a number. If it is an even number, it'll raise the exception. Otherwise, it'll send a message saying invitation is done.*

Demonstration 2

Let us see the complete program now:

```
using static System.Console;

WriteLine("The host is planning a party.");
var inviteTask = Task.Run(() =>
{
    string msg= "Invitation is done.";
    // A dummy logic to generate an exception
    int random =new Random().Next(10);
    if (random % 2 == 0)
    {
        throw new Exception("Some problem occurs.");
    }
    return msg;
}
);

var orderTask = inviteTask.ContinueWith(previousTask =>
{
        WriteLine(previousTask.Result);
```

```
    // Simulating a delay to mimic real-world situation
    Thread.Sleep(1000);
    WriteLine("Food is ordered now.");
  }, TaskContinuationOptions.NotOnFaulted
);

var changePartyDateTask = inviteTask.ContinueWith(previousTask =>
  {
      WriteLine("Party date is shifted due to some
          unavoidable circumstances.");
  }, TaskContinuationOptions.OnlyOnFaulted
);
WriteLine("The host is decorating the house.");
ReadLine();
```

Output

Here is a possible output when there is no exception:

```
The host is planning a party.
The host is decorating the house.
Invitation is done.
Food is ordered now.
```

Here is another possible output where the host needed to shift the party date:

```
The host is planning a party.
The host is decorating the house.
Party date is shifted due to some unavoidable circumstances.
```

Case Study 2

Task continuations help you deal with many different situations. Let me show you one more case study on this topic. Earlier, I told you that continuations can be attached to one or more antecedents. Let us see an example.

This time, I'll use the `ContinueWhenAll` method. As usual, there are many overloads of this method. I am about to use the following one that accepts only two parameters as follows:

```
public Task ContinueWhenAll<TAntecedentResult>
(
  Task<TAntecedentResult>[] tasks,
  Action<Task<TAntecedentResult>[]> continuationAction
)
{
  // Method body is not shown
}
```

Here, the first parameter accepts an array of antecedent tasks (it means that these need to be finished before you continue), and the next parameter is for the `Action` delegate that will execute when all tasks in the array have been completed.

This is why you'll see the following code that indicates that the `orderTask` and the `inviteTask` must be completed before you start a continuation task as follows:

```
var arrangeDinnerTask = Task.Factory.ContinueWhenAll(
    [orderTask,inviteTask],
    tasks =>
    {
        WriteLine("Arranging dinner.");
    }
);
```

POINT TO REMEMBER

You may note that the "Collection expressions" feature in C#12 allows us to write arrangeDinnerTask in this way. If you are using an old version of C#, you may need to write it as follows (notice the change in bold):

```
var arrangeDinnerTask = Task.Factory.ContinueWhenAll(
    new[] { orderTask,inviteTask },
    //[orderTask,inviteTask],  // C#12 onwards
    tasks =>
    {
        WriteLine("Arranging dinner.");
    }
);
```

Demonstration 3

Let us see the complete program now:

```
using static System.Console;

var orderTask = Task.Run(() => WriteLine("Food is ordered."));
var inviteTask = Task.Run(() => WriteLine("Invitation is done."));

var arrangeDinnerTask = Task.Factory.ContinueWhenAll(
    //new[] { orderTask,inviteTask },
    [orderTask,inviteTask],  // C#12 onwards
    tasks =>
    {
        WriteLine("Arranging dinner.");
    }
);

ReadLine();
```

Output

Here is a possible output where food is ordered at the beginning:

```
Food is ordered.
Invitation is done.
Arranging dinner.
```

Here is another possible output where the invitation is done at the beginning:

```
Invitation is done.
Food is ordered.
Arranging dinner.
```

Analysis

In every case, you can see that dinner has been arranged only after the task of ordering food is completed and invitations are done.

Case Study 3

Let us analyze one more case study where you continue a task if any one of the previous tasks completes the execution. In this case, you can use ContinueWhenAny (instead of ContinueWhenAll). For example, here is a sample output that I received when I replaced the ContinueWhenAll method with the ContinueWhenAny method in the previous code:

```
Food is ordered.
Arranging dinner.
Invitation is done.
```

This output shows that dinner was arranged even before the invitations were completed. You may increase the probability of seeing this output by introducing a sleep statement inside inviteTask as follows:

```
var inviteTask = Task.Run(() =>
{
    Thread.Sleep(3000);
    WriteLine("Invitation is done.");
}
);
```

Note   You can also download the **Chapter3_Demo3_CaseStudy3** project to exercise this case study.

Identifying a Task and Its Status

When you work with several tasks in a multithreaded environment, it is necessary to identify the tasks along with the status. Using Task. CurrentId, you can get the ID of the currently executing task.

POINT TO NOTE

CurrentId is used to get the identifier of the currently executing task from the code that the task is executing. However, it is a static property, and it differs from the Id property. Id returns the identifier of a particular Task instance. Attempting to retrieve the CurrentId value from outside the code that a task is executing results a null return.

The life cycle of a Task instance passes through various stages. The Status property is used to verify the current state. On investigation, you'll see that it returns TaskStatus which is an enum type and it has many members. Let me take a snapshot from Visual Studio to show them (see Figure 3-2).

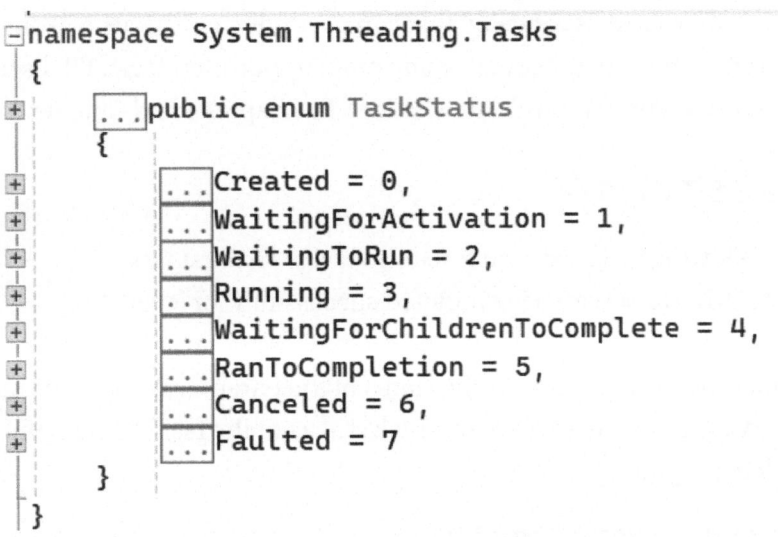

```
namespace System.Threading.Tasks
{
    ... public enum TaskStatus
    {
        ... Created = 0,
        ... WaitingForActivation = 1,
        ... WaitingToRun = 2,
        ... Running = 3,
        ... WaitingForChildrenToComplete = 4,
        ... RanToCompletion = 5,
        ... Canceled = 6,
        ... Faulted = 7
    }
}
```

Figure 3-2. *Different possible states of a Task instance*

In a concurrent environment, it is possible that by the time you receive the value of a task status, the status is changed. However, the interesting point is that once a state is reached, it does not go back to a previous state. For example, once a task reaches a final state, it cannot go back to the Created state. Interestingly, there are three possible final states as follows:

- RanToCompletion

- Canceled

- Faulted

As per their names, these states have their usual meaning. For example, RanToCompletion indicates that the task was completed successfully. Similarly, Faulted indicates the task completed due to an unhandled exception. I assume that I need not mention that Canceled

53

indicates that a task is canceled that can occur due to various reasons such as user intervention, timeouts, or any other application logic. I'll discuss more about exceptions and cancellations in Chapter 4 and Chapter 5.

Demonstration 4

In the following program, you'll see two tasks. The first task (doSomethingTask) can be completed successfully, or it can be encountered with an exception. The second task (statusCheckerTask) is a continuation task that checks the status of the parent task using the Status property (it helps you retrieve the TaskStatus of the task). Here is the complete program:

```
using static System.Console;

var doSomethingTask = Task.Run(
    () =>
        {
            WriteLine($"The task [id:{Task.CurrentId}]
                starts...");
            // Do Something else, if required
            int random = new Random().Next(2);
            WriteLine($"The random number is:{random}");
            // The random number 0 causes the exception
            if (random == 0)
            {
                throw new Exception("Got a zero");
            }
            WriteLine($"The task [id:{Task.CurrentId}] has
                finished.");
        }
    );
```

```
var statusCheckerTask = doSomethingTask.
ContinueWith(previousTask =>
{
    WriteLine($"The task {previousTask.Id}'s status is:
    {previousTask.Status}");
}, TaskContinuationOptions.AttachedToParent
);

ReadKey();
```

Output

Here is a sample output:

```
The task [id:8] starts...
The random number is:0
The task 8's status is: Faulted
```

Here is another sample output:

```
The task [id:8] starts...
The random number is:1
The task [id:8] has finished.
The task 8's status is: RanToCompletion
```

Analysis

If needed, you can modify this program where you use separate branches to handle different scenarios (similar to Demonstration 2). To illustrate the previous line, let me replace the statusCheckerTask with the following blocks of code that handle two possible branches (notice the key changes in bold)):

```
var normalHandlerTask = doSomethingTask.
ContinueWith(previousTask =>
```

```
{
    WriteLine($"The task {previousTask.Id}'s status is:
    {previousTask.Status}");
}, TaskContinuationOptions.AttachedToParent |
   TaskContinuationOptions.NotOnFaulted
);

var faultHandlerTask = doSomethingTask.
ContinueWith(previousTask =>
{
    WriteLine($"The parent task was not completed due to an
    exception.");
},  TaskContinuationOptions.AttachedToParent |
   TaskContinuationOptions.OnlyOnFaulted
);
```

Let's run this modified program. This time, you'll see separate messages based on the task's completion status. Here is the output when the parent task encountered the exception:

```
The task [id:7] starts...
The random number is:0
The parent task was not completed due to an exception.
```

Here is another output when the parent task did not encounter the exception:

```
The task [id:8] starts...
The random number is:1
The task [id:8] has finished.
The task 8's status is: RanToCompletion
```

Q&A Session

Q3.1 In the previous outputs, I see the ID of the parent task is 7 or 8. Looks like, many other tasks were also running along with it. Is this correct?

Yes, I ran this code in VS2022 with the default settings in the debug configuration where the hot reload was enabled. I asked the same question at https://stackoverflow.com/questions/77726578/vs2022-versus-vs2019-how-why-are-the-additional-tasks-being-created and received the answer. If you run the same code in the release configuration (or disable the "hot reload" setting), you can see the lower id as follows:

```
The task [id:1] started doing something...
The random number is:0
The task 1's status is: Faulted
```

Author's note: To choose your preferred configuration, you can follow these steps: right-click the **Solution Explorer** ➤ **Configuration Manager...** ➤ choose **Debug** or **Release** configuration for the project(s).

POINT TO REMEMBER

I often execute my programs in debug mode. So, to see the lower task IDs such as 1, 2, 3, and so forth in the output, I often run those programs with the "hot reload" setting disabled.

Q3.2 Are the task identifiers unique?

Microsoft does not guarantee this. The online link https://learn.microsoft.com/en-us/dotnet/api/system.threading.tasks.task.currentid?view=net-9.0 states the following:

Note that although collisions are very rare, task identifiers are not guaranteed to be unique.

Nested Tasks

Tasks can be nested. It means that you can create a task in the user delegate of another task. The outer task in which the child task is created is often referred to as the parent task. A child task can be any of the following types:

- **Attached**: Created with the `TaskCreationOptions.AttachedToParent` option (if the parent task allows this to be attached)

- **Detached**: Executes independently

Detached Nested Task

Let us start our discussion with detached nested tasks.

Demonstration 5

The following code creates two `Task` instances, called `parent` and `child`. Notice that the `child` task is created inside the `parent` task. However, I did not attach the child task to the parent. This is why you see the line `,TaskCreationOptions.AttachedToParent` is commented in the following code.

POINT TO NOTE

The `Task.Factory.StartNew` method has the overload that accepts `TaskCreationOptions` as a parameter. The same is not available for the `Task.Run` method.

```
using static System.Console;

var parent = Task.Factory.StartNew(
    () =>
    {
        WriteLine($"The parent task has started.");

        var child = Task.Factory.StartNew(
            () =>
            {
                WriteLine("The child task has started.");
                // Forcing some delay
                Thread.Sleep(1000);
                WriteLine("The child task has finished.");
            }
            //,TaskCreationOptions.AttachedToParent
            );
    }
);
Thread.Sleep(5);
parent.Wait();
WriteLine($"The parent task has finished now.");
```

Output

Here is a sample output from my computer:

```
The parent task has started.
The child task has started.
The parent task has finished now.
```

You can see that this output reflects that the child task was started, but it does not reflect whether it was finished. This is because I created the child task without using TaskCreationOptions.AttachedToParent option.

So, it becomes a detached child task that executes independently of its parent. This is why the parent task does not care whether the child task is completed.

Q&A Session

Q3.3 I understand that in the previous demonstration, you waited only for the parent task to complete but not for the child task. So, if I replace the line parent.Wait(); **with the line** Task.WaitAll(parent, child); **I can see whether the child task finishes its execution. Am I right?**

No. In that code sample, the child task was nested. So, it was not in the scope. So, your proposed code will cause the following compile-time error:

CS0103 The name 'child' does not exist in the current context

Q3.4 In the previous program, you used a Sleep statement in the main thread. Was it necessary?

Nice catch. Indeed, it was not necessary. However, by placing this Sleep statement, I increase the probability of showing the line "The child task has started." in the output.

Attached Nested Task

Let us uncomment the line //,TaskCreationOptions.AttachedToParent in the previous code and execute the program again. This time, you must see the completion status of the child task. Here is a sample output for you:

```
The parent task has started.
The child task has started.
The child task has finished.
The parent task has finished now.
```

POINTS TO NOTE

You can attach a child task to the parent task if and only if the parent task allows you to do this. In this context, you can note the following two points from the official documentation (see `https://learn.microsoft.com/en-us/dotnet/standard/parallel-programming/attached-and-detached-child-tasks`):

1. Parent tasks can explicitly prevent child tasks from attaching to them by specifying the `TaskCreationOptions.DenyChildAttach` option in the parent task's class constructor or the `TaskFactory.StartNew` method.

2. Parent tasks implicitly prevent child tasks from attaching to them if they are created by calling the `Task.Run` method.

Q&A Session

Q3.5 I have a doubt: In the previous demonstration (Demonstration 5), you have only written `parent.Wait();`. It means that you care about the parent task to be finished, but the same is not true for the child task. As a result, there is no guarantee that the output will reflect whether the child task could finish its execution. Is this a correct understanding?

No. Microsoft has designed the architecture in such a way that if you create a parent–child relationship, waiting on the parent task forces you to wait for the child task to complete.

Forcing Parent Task to Wait

You can force the parent task to wait for the child task to finish (even if it is a detached nested task) by accessing the `Task<TResult>.Result` property of the child task as well. Let us see an example that is placed next.

Demonstration 6

To demonstrate this, I have slightly modified the previous program. For your reference, I have highlighted the new code in bold and commented out the old code as follows:

```csharp
using static System.Console;

var parent = Task.Factory.StartNew(
    () =>
    {
        WriteLine($"The parent task has started.");

        var child = Task.Factory.StartNew(
            () =>
            {
                WriteLine("The child task has started.");
                // Forcing some delay
                Thread.Sleep(1000);
                // WriteLine("The child task has finished.");
                return "the child task has finished.";
            }
            // , TaskCreationOptions.AttachedToParent
            );
        // Parent task now waits for this detached child.
        return child.Result;

    }
);
// Thread.Sleep(5);
// parent.Wait();
// WriteLine($"The parent task has finished now.");
WriteLine($"The parent task confirms that {parent.Result}");
```

Output

Here is the output of this program:

```
The parent task has started.
The child task has started.
The parent task confirms that the child task has finished.
```

Unwrapping Nested Tasks

Let us discuss something more on nested tasks. Consider the following code:

```
var someTask = Task.Factory.StartNew(
    () => Task.Factory.StartNew(() => 200)
);
```

You understand that in this code, someTask is of type **Task<Task<int>>**. Given this code, if you now exercise the following code

```
WriteLine(someTask.Result);
```

you'll see the output System.Threading.Tasks.Task`1[System.Int32].

Starting with .NET 4, you can use one of the Unwrap extension methods to transform any Task<Task<TResult>> to a Task<TResult> (or a Task<Task> to a Task). This new task will represent the inner nested task and include the cancellation state along with the exceptions.

POINTS TO NOTE

The Unwrap method has two overloads:

```
public static Task Unwrap(this Task<Task> task);
public static Task<TResult> Unwrap<TResult>(this
    Task<Task<TResult>> task);
```

You can see that both of these are extension methods. When you unwrap a
Task<Task> (or Task<Task<TResult>>), you get a new task (often called
a **proxy**).

To illustrate, let us see the following code:

```
var someTask1 = Task.Factory.StartNew(
    () => Task.Factory.StartNew(() => 200)
).Unwrap();
WriteLine($"Received: {someTask1.Result}");
```

Once you execute this program, you'll see the following output:

```
Received: 200
```

Interestingly, if you work with the Run method, it can do the same kind
of unwrapping for you. Here is an equivalent code:

```
var someTask2 = Task.Run(
    () => Task.Run(() => 200)
);
WriteLine($"Received: {someTask2.Result}");
```

If you execute this code, you'll see the same output.

Special Note

In this book, I did not discuss async and await keywords. However, in this context, I'd like you to note that you can use the await keyword for unwrapping a layer. For example, the following code will also compile and produce the same output:

```
var someTask3 = Task.Factory.StartNew(
    () => Task.Factory.StartNew(() => 200)
    );
WriteLine($"Received: {await someTask3.Result}");
```

Note   Download the project Chapter3_Demo_UnwrappingNestedTasks to experiment these code segments. You can find this project in the Chapter3 folder.

Summary

This chapter discussed task continuations and nested tasks. In brief, it answered the following questions:

- How can you implement a simple task continuation mechanism?

- How can you create branches to employ a conditional continuation mechanism?

- How can you check the status of the current task?

- How can you create, manage, and unwrap a nested task?

Exercises

Check your understanding by attempting the following exercises (you do not need to handle exceptions or cancellations for these exercises):

REMINDER

As said before, you can safely assume that all other necessary namespaces are available for these code segments. The same comment applies to all exercises in this book as well.

E3.1 Starting with C# 12, we can define a primary constructor as a part of the class declaration. Here is an example:

```
class Employee (string name, int id)
{
    private string _name=name;
    private int _id = id;
    public override string ToString()
    {
        return $"Name:{_name} Id:{_id}";
    }
}
```

You can create an instance of the Employee class as follows:

```
Employee emp = new("Bob", 1);
```

Now, assume that there are two tasks where the first task will create an Employee instance. The second task will follow the first task and perform the following things: first, it will verify whether the first task completes the process successfully. Next, it will print the current date and time. Can you write a program fulfilling the criteria?

E3.2 Create a background task that pings a URL (say www.google.com). Then, create a continuation task that shows the result to the console. (Assume that your computer is already connected to the Internet.)

E3.3 Can you predict the output of the following program?

```
using static System.Console;

var helloTask = Task.Run(() =>
{
    WriteLine("Hello reader!");
    var aboutTask = Task.Factory.StartNew(() =>
    {
        Task.Delay(1000);
        WriteLine("How are you?");
    }, TaskCreationOptions.AttachedToParent);
});

helloTask.Wait();
```

E3.4 Can you compile the following code?

```
using static System.Console;
var someTask = Task.Factory.StartNew(
    () => Task.Run(() => 300)
).Unwrap();
WriteLine($"Received: {someTask.Result}");
```

E3.5 Can you predict the following output of the following program?

```
using static System.Console;
var getGift = Task.Factory.StartNew(() => "Sunny wins a book")
    .ContinueWith(previousTask =>
      Task.Run(() => previousTask.Result+" and a laptop."))
    .Unwrap();
WriteLine(getGift.Result);
```

Solutions to Exercises

Here is a sample solution set for the exercises in this chapter.

E3.1

Here is a sample program based on the features that you learned in this chapter:

```
using static System.Console;

var createEmp = Task.Factory.StartNew(
    () =>
    {
        Employee emp = new("Bob", 1);
        WriteLine($"Created an employee with {emp}");
    }
    )
    .ContinueWith(
      task =>
      {
          WriteLine($"Was the previous task completed?
            { task.IsCompletedSuccessfully} ");
          WriteLine($"Current time:{DateTime.Now}");
      }
    );

createEmp.Wait();

class Employee (string name, int id)
{
    private string _name = name;
    private int _id = id;
```

```
public override string ToString()
{
    return $"Name: {_name} Id: {_id}";
}
}
```

Here is a sample output:

```
Created an employee with Name: Bob Id: 1
Was the previous task completed?  True
Current time:10/16/2024 9:58:08 AM
```

E3.2

Here is a sample program that fulfills the criteria:

```
using static System.Console;
using System.Net.NetworkInformation;

string url ="www.google.com";
WriteLine($"The main thread initiates a task that starts
pinging {url}");
var pingTask = Task.Run(() => new Ping().Send(url));
var statusTask = pingTask.ContinueWith(previousTask =>
 {
   WriteLine($"Ping Status of {url}: {pingTask.Result.
   Status}");
 }
);
WriteLine($"The main thread is ready to do other work.");
statusTask.Wait();
```

Here is a sample output:

```
The main thread initiates a task that starts pinging
www.google.com
The main thread is ready to do other work.
Ping Status of www.google.com: Success
```

Alternative Code:

Let me show you one more solution where you can avoid using the variable statusTask and write a compact version of the previous program as follows:

```
// There is no change in the previous code
WriteLine($"The main thread initiates a task that starts
pinging {url}");
```

```
var pingTask = Task.Run(() => new Ping().Send(url))
    .ContinueWith(previousTask => previousTask.Result.Status);
WriteLine($"The main thread is ready to do other work.");
WriteLine($"Ping Status of {url}: {pingTask.Result}");
```

Author's note: You can see that the main thread was not blocked while executing the background task. It was blocked at the end for displaying the output of the program. However, by this time, it completed its remaining job. Once you download the project Chapter3_Ex3.2, you can exercise both solutions.

E3.3

On my computer, this program often shows the following output:

```
Hello reader!
```

It is because the application terminated before the aboutTask finishes its execution. Using the ReadKey() or ReadLine() method at the end of the main thread, you can hold the control until you see the following output:

```
Hello reader!
How are you?
```

You may wonder about this. However, notice that to create the parent task, I have used the Run method but not the StartNew method. So, if you use the StartNew method instead of the Run method as follows:

```
using static System.Console;

//var helloTask = Task.Run(() =>
var helloTask = Task.Factory.StartNew(() =>
{
 // There is no change in the remaining code
```

you can expect to see the following output for sure:

```
Hello reader!
How are you?
```

In this context, I'd like you to remember that Task.Run(someAction) is functionally equivalent to the following:

```
Task.Factory.StartNew(
someAction,
CancellationToken.None,
TaskCreationOptions.DenyChildAttach,
TaskScheduler.Default);
```

It means that Task.Run by default does not allow child tasks to be attached to the parent task. However, StartNew(Action, CancellationToken) allows this activity.

71

E3.4

Yes. You should see the following output:

```
Received: 300
```

E3.5

Here is the output:

```
Sunny wins a book and a laptop.
```

CHAPTER 4

Exception Handling

It is no surprise that tasks can encounter exceptions. It is also true that different tasks may throw different exceptions. In a multithreaded environment, handling these exceptions can be tricky as well as challenging. Your application must respond to them gracefully to avoid unwanted crashes and maintain stability. This is why exception handling is essential for building reliable and robust applications. This chapter focuses on this topic.

Understanding the Challenge

Since you are reading the advanced concepts of programming, I assume that you are familiar with the fundamentals of exceptions and how to handle them in a C# program. This is why I'll not discuss those basics in this book. Instead, I'll focus on possible exceptional scenarios that can be raised when you perform task programming in a multithreaded environment.

The Program That Does Not Show Exceptions

If the symptoms are prominent, the doctor can understand the problem of the patient easily. However, unobserved problems are hard to detect. The same is true for programming. An unobserved exception can cause lots of problems. To illustrate, let's see the following program in which the main thread creates a task that raises an exception that does not appear in the output. (Based on your Visual Studio settings, you may see the highlighted

© Vaskaran Sarcar 2025
V. Sarcar, *Task Programming in C# and .NET*, Apress Pocket Guides,
https://doi.org/10.1007/979-8-8688-1279-8_4

line that raises the exception. However, if you continue the execution (by pressing F5 or the Continue button), you'll not see any information about this exception in the output.

MICROSOFT'S NOTE FOR VISUAL STUDIO USERS

If you are a Visual Studio user and write programs that deal with multiple cancellation requests, I want you to remember the following note from Microsoft (`https://learn.microsoft.com/en-us/dotnet/standard/threading/how-to-listen-for-multiple-cancellation-requests`):

When "Just My Code" is enabled, Visual Studio in some cases will break on the line that throws the exception and display an error message that says "exception not handled by user code." This error is benign. You can press F5 to continue from it.

It keeps saying the following:

To prevent Visual Studio from breaking on the first error, just uncheck the "Just My Code" checkbox under Tools, Options, Debugging, General.

Demonstration 1

Let us execute the program:

```
using static System.Console;

WriteLine("The main thread starts executing.");

try
{
  var validateUserTask = Task.Run(() =>
    throw new UnauthorizedAccessException("Unauthorized user.")
  );
}
```

```
catch (Exception e)
{
    WriteLine($"Caught error: {e.Message}");
}

WriteLine("End of the program.");
```

Output

Upon executing this program, you'll see the following output:

```
The main thread starts executing.
End of the program.
```

The output does not show anything about the exception. Why? Notice that in this program, the main thread did not encounter the exception; it was encountered by validateUserTask which was created by this main thread.

Since the unobserved exceptions can cause problems at a later stage, you'd like to see and handle them as per the priority.

Introducing AggregateException

How could you get the information about the exception? An obvious way is handling the exception inside the task itself. For example, I can redefine the task as follows:

```
var validateUserTask = Task.Run(
    () =>
    {
        string msg = string.Empty;
        try
```

```
  {
    throw new UnauthorizedAccessException("Unauthorized
    user.");
  }
  catch (Exception e)
  {
    WriteLine($"Caught error inside the task: {
    e.Message} ");
  }
  return msg;
});
```

How can you get the error detail if the task does not handle the exceptions? Let us investigate the answer.

Demonstration 2

In task-based programming, exceptions are stored in the task object and are not thrown immediately when they occur. If an exception occurs within a task, it is encapsulated within an AggregateException that contains all the exceptions that were thrown during the task's execution. This feature allows you to handle the exceptions collectively or individually.

POINT TO NOTE

The AggregateException belongs to the System namespace. This class inherits from the Exception class.

The AggregateException can be thrown in any of the following scenarios:

- You try to access the task's result.

- You explicitly call the Wait method on the task.

- You await the task. (Since this book does not discuss async and await keywords, I am not discussing this now.)

Now, you understand that in the previous demonstration if you use any of the lines WriteLine(validateUserTask.Result); or validateUserTask.Wait(); inside the try block, you can observe the exception. Here is a sample demonstration where I use the statement validateUserTask.Wait(); inside the try block as follows (notice the change in bold):

```
// There is no change in the previous code

try
{
  var validateUserTask = Task.Run(() =>
    throw new UnauthorizedAccessException("Unauthorized user.")
  );
  validateUserTask.Wait();
}
// There is no change in the remaining code as well
```

Output

Once you execute the program again, you will see the following output:

```
The main thread starts executing.
Caught error: One or more errors occurred. (Unauthorized user.)
End of the program.
```

The output shows the error now. However, you can see that the error information "Unauthorized user." is wrapped as an InnerException.

Q&A Session

Q4.1 In the previous output, the error information "Unauthorized user." is wrapped as an InnerException. What is the reason behind it?

This program caught an AggregateException which is used to consolidate multiple failures into a single, throwable exception object. You see this kind of exception heavily in task programming.

To verify this, you can slightly modify the catch block in the previous demonstration (Demonstration 2) as follows:

```
catch (Exception e)
{
    WriteLine($"Caught error: {e.Message}");
    WriteLine($"Exception name: {e.GetType().Name}");
}
```

If you execute the application again, you will see the following output:

```
The main thread starts executing.
Caught error: One or more errors occurred. (Unauthorized user.)
Exception name: AggregateException
End of the program.
```

Now, you can see that the program caught an AggregateException. The official documentation (see https://learn.microsoft.com/en-us/dotnet/standard/parallel-programming/exception-handling-task-parallel-library) states the following about it:

> *To propagate all the exceptions back to the calling thread, the Task infrastructure wraps them in an AggregateException instance. The AggregateException exception has an InnerExceptions property that can be enumerated to examine all the original exceptions that were thrown, and handle (or not handle) each one individually.*

This is why you see the actual error (Unauthorized user.) was wrapped as an inner exception in the previous output.

POINT TO NOTE

Since the AggregateException helps you to consolidate multiple failures (or errors) in concurrent environments, they are frequently used in task programming. Now onward, you will see me using the AggregateException inside the catch blocks as well.

Strategies to Tackle Exceptions

Till now, we have handled only one exception. It is obvious that your program will deal with many different tasks and each of them can throw different exceptions. So, let's focus on how to handle exceptions that can be caused by one or more tasks.

Before I start this discussion, let me tell you that different programming models have different strategies for exception handling. For example, if you follow object-oriented programming (OOP), you'd like to use try, catch, and finally blocks. However, these are typically absent in functional programming (FP). In my other book *Introducing Functional Programming Using C#*, I had a detailed discussion on this topic. For now, you do not need to investigate those details. Instead, let us concentrate on OOP and simplify the overall strategies by making the following categories:

- Handling possible exceptions in a single location

- Handling possible exceptions in multiple locations

Handling Exceptions in Single Location

Let us start our discussion with the first category, i.e., how to handle the possible exceptions in one place.

Demonstration 3

This program creates two different tasks inside the main thread. Each of these tasks raises an exception. Here, I pass through the inner exceptions and display the error details. Go through the complete program now:

```
using static System.Console;
WriteLine("Exception handling demo.");

try
{
    var validateUserTask = Task.Run(
      () =>
        {
            // Some other code, if any
            throw new UnauthorizedAccessException("Unauthorized
            user.");
        }
    );
    var storeDataTask = Task.Run(
      () =>
      {
          // Some other code, if any
          throw new InsufficientMemoryException("Insufficient
          memory.");
      }
    );
```

```
    Task.WaitAll(validateUserTask, storeDataTask);
}
catch (AggregateException ae)
{
    foreach (Exception e in ae.InnerExceptions)
    {
        WriteLine($"Caught error: {e.Message}");
    }
}
```

Output

Here is a sample output from this program:

```
Exception handling demo.
Caught error: Unauthorized user.
Caught error: Insufficient memory.
```

This is a very common approach for exception handling in task programming. Now, let me show you two more approaches that can be used in a similar context.

Alternative Approach-1

Notice the catch block in Demonstration 3. You can see that I used ae. InnerExceptions to display the errors in the output. Here is an alternative version where **I flatten the inner instances and then start traversing the exceptions** as follows:

```
catch (AggregateException ae)
{
    // Alternative approach-1
    var exceptions = ae.Flatten().InnerExceptions;
    foreach (Exception e in exceptions)
```

```
    {
        WriteLine($"Caught error: {e.Message}");
    }
}
```

Alternative Approach-2

In the AggregateException class, you can see a method called Handle which has the following form:

```
public void Handle(Func<Exception, bool> predicate)
{
 // The method body is not shown
}
```

Using this method, you can invoke a handler on each exception contained in an AggregateException. To illustrate, this time let me rewrite the catch block in the previous demonstration as follows (I have kept other approaches in the commented code for your immediate reference):

```
catch (AggregateException ae)
{
    //// Initial approach
    //foreach (Exception e in ae.InnerExceptions)
    //{
    //    WriteLine($"Caught error: {e.Message}");
    //}

    //// Alternative approach-1
    //var exceptions = ae.Flatten().InnerExceptions;
    //foreach (Exception e in exceptions)
    //{
    //    WriteLine($"Caught error: {e.Message}");
    //}
```

```
// Alternative approach-2
ae.Handle(e =>
{
    WriteLine($"Caught error: {e.Message}");
    return true;
});
}
```

By executing the program now, you can get the same output.

Note   In the Chapter4_Demo3 project, you will see all the different approaches that I discussed so far. There you'll see that alternative codes are commented out for easy comparison. By downloading the project, you can play with these approaches.

Q&A Session

Q4.2 I can see that you have thrown two different exceptions from two different tasks. How can I distinguish them?

It is easy. You can associate the task IDs or an appropriate message with the exception's Source property. Here is a sample program that is created by slightly modifying Demonstration 3 (notice the changes in bold):

```
using static System.Console;
WriteLine("Exception handling demo.");

try
{
    var validateUserTask = Task.Run(
      () =>
```

```
        {
            // Some other code, if any
            throw new UnauthorizedAccessException("Unauthoriz
            ed user.")
            { Source = "validateUserTask" };
        }
        );
    var storeDataTask = Task.Run(
        () =>
        {
            // Some other code, if any
            throw new InsufficientMemoryException("Insufficient
            memory.")
            { Source = "storeDataTask" };
        }
        );

    Task.WaitAll(validateUserTask, storeDataTask);
}
// Initial approach
catch (AggregateException ae)
{
    // Initial approach
    foreach (Exception e in ae.InnerExceptions)
    {
        // WriteLine($"Caught error: {e.Message}");
        WriteLine($"The task: {e.Source} raised {e.GetType()}:
        {e.Message}");
    }
}
```

Here is a sample output that I got by running this modified program:

```
Exception handling demo.
The task: validateUserTask raised System.
    UnauthorizedAccessException: Unauthorized user.
The task: storeDataTask raised System.
    InsufficientMemoryException: Insufficient memory.
```

Q4.3 It appears to me that I can follow the same approach if multiple tasks throw the same exception as well. Is this correct?

Yes, you got it right.

Handling Exceptions in Multiple Locations

I assume that you have got the idea of handling multiple exceptions. This is OK and probably the most common approach. Next, I will show you a mechanism where you handle one part of the aggregate exception in one place and the remaining part in another place. More specifically, you propagate the remaining part of the exception(s) up to the hierarchy and handle it there. I am discussing this to show you the effectiveness of the Handle method.

First, I want you to focus on the following code fragment (it is taken from the upcoming demonstration). This code fragment says that you'd like to handle only the InsufficientMemoryException but no other exceptions in this location. This is why the if block returns true here:

```
// Some code before
catch (AggregateException ae)
{
    // Handling only InsufficientMemoryException, other
    // exceptions will be propagated up to the hierarchy
    ae.Handle(
        e =>
```

```
    {
        if (e is InsufficientMemoryException)
        {
            WriteLine($"Caught error inside InvokeTasks():
            {e.Message}");
            return true;
        }
        else
        {
            return false;
        }
    }
);
}
```

Demonstration 4

Let us see a complete program now. In the upcoming program, the main thread calls the InvokeTasks method that in turn creates and runs three tasks. The first two tasks (validateUserTask and storeDataTask) are already shown in the previous demonstration. You know that these tasks will raise exceptions. *The third task, named useDllTask, is added for the sake of discussion, so that you do not assume that you need to handle an equal number of tasks in each location.*

You'll see that I catch all the possible sets of exceptions inside InvokeTasks but handled only one of them: InsufficientMemoryException. As a result, the remaining exceptions will be passed up to the calling hierarchy. This is why you'll see me handling them inside the main thread. Let's see the complete program now:

```
using static System.Console;

WriteLine("Exception handling demo.");
try
{
    InvokeTasks();
}
catch (AggregateException ae)
{
    ae.Handle(e =>
    {
        WriteLine($"Caught error inside Main(): {e.Message}");
        return true;
    });
}

static void InvokeTasks()
{
    try
    {
        var validateUserTask = Task.Run(
            () =>
            {
                // Some other code, if any
                throw new UnauthorizedAccessException
                ("Unauthorized user.");
            }
        );
        var storeDataTask = Task.Run(
            () =>
```

```
    {
      // Some other code, if any
      throw new InsufficientMemoryException("Insufficient
      memory.");
    }
    );

    var useDllTask = Task.Run(
      () =>
      {
        // Some other code, if any
        throw new DllNotFoundException("The required dll is
        missing!");
      }
    );

    Task.WaitAll(validateUserTask, storeDataTask,
    useDllTask);
  }
  // The catch block is placed here. To avoid repetitions,
  // it is not shown again.
}
```

Note   To avoid repetitions, I did not show you the **catch** block inside the **InvokeTasks** method again. You can download the complete program from the Apress website.

Output

Here is a sample output from this program:

```
Exception handling demo.
Caught error inside InvokeTasks(): Insufficient memory.
Caught error inside Main(): Unauthorized user.
Caught error inside Main(): The required dll is missing!
```

Q&A Session

Q4.4 I understand that I can handle exceptions in different ways. However, I'd like to know whether there is any general guideline for handling exceptions in a concurrent environment.

Normally, experts suggest that if you do not handle exceptions within tasks, you should try to handle them as closely as possible, particularly, to those places where you wait for the task completion or retrieve the result of the task invocation. I try to follow this guideline as well.

Summary

This chapter continued the discussion on task programming, but this time, the focus was on handling exceptions with different examples and case studies. In brief, it answered the following questions:

- What is AggregateException and why is it important in task programming?

- How can you display the exceptions that can be thrown by different tasks?

- How can you flatten the inner instances of exceptions?

- How can you handle all the possible exceptions together?

- How can you handle possible exceptions in separate locations?

Exercises

Check your understanding by attempting the following exercises:

REMINDER

As said before, you can safely assume that all other necessary namespaces are available for these code segments. The same comment applies to all exercises in this book as well.

E4.1 If you execute the following code, can you predict the output?

```
using static System.Console;
WriteLine("Exercise 4.1");
try
{
    int b = 0;
    Task<int> value = Task.Run(() => 25 / b);
}
catch (Exception e)
{
    WriteLine($"Caught: {e.GetType()}, Message: {e.Message}");
}
WriteLine("End");
```

E4.2 If you execute the following code, can you predict the output?

```
using static System.Console;
WriteLine("Exercise 4.2 and Exercise 4.3");

try
{
    DoSomething();
}
catch (AggregateException ae)
{
    ae.Handle(
        e =>
        {
            WriteLine($"Caught inside main: {e.Message}");
            return true;
        }
    );
}
static void DoSomething()
{
    try
    {
      var task1 = Task.Run(() => throw new
      InvalidDataException("invalid data"));
      var task2 = Task.Run(() => throw new
      OutOfMemoryException("insufficient memory"));
        // For Exercise 4.2
        Task.WaitAll(task1, task2);
        // For Exercise 4.3
        // task1.Wait();
        // task2.Wait();
    }
```

```
    catch (AggregateException ae)
    {
        ae.Handle(
            e =>
            {
                if (e is InvalidDataException)
                {
                    WriteLine($"The DoSomething method
                    encounters:
                    {e.Message}");
                    return true;
                }
                else
                {
                    return false;
                }
            }
        );
    }
}
```

E4.3 In the previous program, replace the line:

```
Task.WaitAll(task1, task2);
```

with the following lines:

```
task1.Wait();
task2.Wait();
```

Can you predict the output?

E4.4 If you execute the following code, can you predict the output?

```
using static System.Console;
WriteLine("Exercise 4.4");
```

CHAPTER 4   EXCEPTION HANDLING

```
try
{
    int b = 0;
    var task1 = Task.Run(() => throw new
     InvalidOperationException("invalid operation"));
    var task2 = Task.Run(() => 5/b);
    Task.WaitAny(task1, task2);
    WriteLine("End");
}
catch (AggregateException ae)
{
    ae.Handle(e =>
    {
        if (e is InvalidOperationException |
            e is DivideByZeroException )
        {
            WriteLine($"Caught error: {e.Message}");
            return true;
        }
        return false;
    }
    );
}
```

E4.5 Can you predict the following output of the following program?

```
using static System.Console;
WriteLine("Exercise 4.5");
var errorTask = Task.Run(() => throw new Exception("unwanted
    situation"));
var outerTask = Task.Factory.StartNew(() => errorTask);
while (!outerTask.IsCompleted) { Thread.Sleep(10); }
```

```
WriteLine($"The status of the outer task is: {outerTask.
    Status}");
while (!outerTask.Unwrap().IsCompleted) { Thread.Sleep(10); }
WriteLine($"The status of the inner task is: {outerTask.
    Unwrap().Status}");
```

Solutions to Exercises

Here is a sample solution set for the exercises in this chapter.

E4.1

This program produces the following output:

```
Exercise 4.1
End
```

Author's note: You do not observe the exception because the main thread did not encounter the exception; it was encountered by the task that was created by this main thread.

To see the exception, you can modify the try block as follows (the change is shown in bold):

```
// There is no change in the previous code
try
{
    int b = 0;
    Task<int> value = Task.Run(() => 25 / b);
    WriteLine(value.Result);
}
// There is no change in the remaining code as well
```

You'll see the following output:

```
Exercise 4.1
Caught: System.AggregateException, Message: One or more errors
    occurred. (Attempted to divide by zero.)
End
```

Notice that instead of seeing the System.DivideByZeroException, you are seeing the System.AggregateException in this output. You know that this is the expected result of this program.

E4.2

The program produces the following output:

```
Exercise 4.2 and Exercise 4.3
The DoSomething method encounters: invalid data
Caught inside main: insufficient memory
```

E4.3

The call to the statement task1.Wait(); causes the InvalidDataException. As a result, control leaves the try block and produces the following output:

```
Exercise 4.2 and Exercise 4.3
The DoSomething method encounters: invalid data
```

E4.4

This program produces the following output:

```
Exercise 4.4
End
```

You may be wondering why you are not seeing the task's exception(s) in the output. It is because when you use the WaitAny method, the task's exception does not propagate to the AggregateException. I encourage you to read Stephen Clearly's nice blog post (see https://blog. stephencleary.com/2014/10/a-tour-of-task-part-5-wait.html) that summarizes the difference between WaitAny and WaitAll (or Wait) as follows:

> *The semantics of WaitAny are a bit different than WaitAll and Wait: WaitAny merely waits for the first task to complete. It will not propagate that task's exception in an AggregateException. Rather, any task failures will need to be checked after WaitAny returns. WaitAny will return -1 on timeout, and will throw OperationCanceledException if the wait is cancelled.*

Author's note: Still, if you like to see the exception detail in the output, you can slightly modify the try block as follows (the changes are shown in bold):

```
// There is no change in the previous code
try
{
    int b = 0;
    var task1 = Task.Run(() => throw new
        InvalidOperationException("invalid operation"));
    var task2 = Task.Run(() => 5 / b);
    // Task.WaitAny(task1, task2);
    var tasks = new[]{ task1, task2 };
    int taskIndex = Task.WaitAny(tasks);
    tasks[taskIndex].Wait();
    WriteLine("End");
}
```

```
// There is no change in the remaining code
```

Here is a sample output once you run this modified program:

```
Exercise 4.4
Caught error: invalid operation
```

E4.5

Here is the output:

```
Exercise 4.5
The status of the outer task is: RanToCompletion
The status of the inner task is: Faulted
```

CHAPTER 5

Managing Cancellations

Cancellation is an essential mechanism in task programming. It is helpful in any of the following scenarios:

- Stopping a running task gracefully when it is no longer needed

- Freeing up a critical resource

- Improving the application's responsiveness

This is why a long-running task may regularly check whether a cancellation request has been raised. If so, it must respond to that request accordingly.

However, having the task cancellation capability does not encourage you to abruptly stop a task, as that can leave the application in an inconsistent state. Instead, you make a cooperative model where the task and the calling code (that initiates the cancellation) can work together. This chapter focuses on this topic.

© Vaskaran Sarcar 2025
V. Sarcar, *Task Programming in C# and .NET*, Apress Pocket Guides,
https://doi.org/10.1007/979-8-8688-1279-8_5

Prerequisites

To manage task cancellations in C#, you must be familiar with the following:

- **CancellationTokenSource**: This class is responsible for signaling the cancellation. It generates a CancellationToken that is passed to the task to monitor the cancellation requests.

- **CancellationToken**: This is a struct that is passed to the task and provides a way to check if cancellation has been requested. This token is used to propagate the notification for a task cancellation.

Let us see how to use them in your program. First, you use the following lines of code:

```
CancellationTokenSource tokenSource = new();
CancellationToken token = tokenSource.Token;
```

Obviously, using the var keyword, you can write an equivalent code as follows:

```
var tokenSource = new CancellationTokenSource();
var token = tokenSource.Token;
```

Next, you pass this token to the intended task. Earlier, you saw (in Figure 2-1 in Chapter 2) that the Task constructor has several overloaded versions. Some of them accept a CancellationToken instance as a method parameter. Here is an example:

```
public Task(Action action, CancellationToken cancellationToken);
```

The StartNew method of the TaskFactory class and the Run method of the Task class have similar overloads. Here are a few more examples for your reference:

```
public Task StartNew(Action action, CancellationToken
    cancellationToken)
public static Task Run(Action action, CancellationToken
    cancellationToken)
public static Task<TResult> Run<TResult>(Func<TResult> function,
    CancellationToken cancellationToken)
```

These constructs give you a clue on how to pass a cancellation token to a task. For your immediate reference, let me show you the following code that is used in the upcoming example:

```
var printTask = Task.Run
 (
  () =>
  {
     // Some code not shown here
  }, token
);
```

However, you must remember the following guidelines from Microsoft (see https://learn.microsoft.com/en-us/dotnet/standard/parallel-programming/how-to-cancel-a-task-and-its-children):

> *The calling thread does not forcibly end the task; it only signals that cancellation is requested. If the task is already running, it is up to the user delegate to notice the request and respond appropriately.*

Note   This prior message indicates that it is possible that by the time a calling thread raises a cancellation request, the running task finishes its execution. So, if you want to cancel a running task, you should raise the cancellation request as soon as possible.

User-Initiated Cancellations

A cancellation request is often raised by users. You can also initiate an automated cancellation after a certain time interval. Let us start our discussion with the user-initiated cancellations.

Initial Approach

In the first approach, you evaluate an `if` condition before raising the cancellation request. If needed, you can do some additional work before you cancel the task. For example, you can introduce a message saying that this task is about to be canceled. You can also clean up the necessary resources as well before you cancel the task. Finally, you put a `break` or `return` statement to exit from the particular block of code. Probably, most of us are aware of this kind of **soft exit mechanism**. Let me show you an example.

Demonstration 1

In the upcoming demonstration, I created a task that can keep printing the numbers from 0 to 99. Since I'd like to provide support for cancellation, you'll see me instantiating a `CancellationTokenSource` object to generate a cancellation token and pass it to the task to raise the cancellation request. Here is the complete program:

Note   Nowadays, computer processors are very fast. So, this task can finish its execution very fast. To prevent this, I impose a short sleep after it prints a number.

```csharp
using static System.Console;

WriteLine("Simple cancellation demonstration.");

var tokenSource = new CancellationTokenSource();
var token = tokenSource.Token;

var printTask = Task.Run
  (
    () =>
    {
        // A loop that runs 100 times
        for (int i = 0; i < 100; i++)
        {
            // Approach - 1
            if (token.IsCancellationRequested)
            {
                WriteLine("Cancelling the print activity.");
                // Do some cleanups, if required
                return;
            }

            WriteLine($"{i}");
            // Imposing the sleep to make some delay
            Thread.Sleep(500);
        }
    }, token
  );
```

```
WriteLine("Enter c to cancel the task.");
char ch = ReadKey().KeyChar;
if (ch.Equals('c'))
{
    WriteLine("\nRaising the cancellation request.");
    tokenSource.Cancel();
}
try
{
    printTask.Wait();
    //printTask.Wait(token); // This line will be used later
}
catch (OperationCanceledException oce)
{
    WriteLine($"Operation canceled. Message: {oce.Message}");
}
catch (AggregateException ae)
{
    foreach (Exception e in ae.InnerExceptions)
    {
        WriteLine($"Caught: {e.GetType()}, Message:
        {e.Message}");
    }
}

WriteLine($"The final status of printTask is: {printTask.Status}");
WriteLine("End of the main thread.");
```

Output

Here is a sample output when I triggered the cancellation request by pressing "c" from my keyboard:

```
Simple cancellation demonstration.
Enter c to cancel the task.
0
1
2
3
c
Raising the cancellation request.
Cancelling the print activity.
The final status of printTask is: RanToCompletion
End of the main thread.
```

Q&A Session

Q5.1 In the previous demonstration, you canceled the task, but in the output, the final status of the task was displayed as RanToCompletion, instead of Canceled. Is this a bug?

No. Let us see what Microsoft says about it. The online documentation link https://learn.microsoft.com/en-us/dotnet/standard/parallel-programming/task-cancellation states the following:

> *A successful cancellation involves the requesting code calling the CancellationTokenSource.Cancel method and the user delegate terminating the operation in a timely manner. You can terminate the operation by using one of these options:*

- By returning from the delegate. In many scenarios, this option is sufficient. However, a task instance that's canceled in this way transitions to the TaskStatus. RanToCompletion state, not to the TaskStatus.Canceled state.

- By throwing an OperationCanceledException and passing it the token on which cancellation was requested. The preferred way to perform this is to use the ThrowIfCancellationRequested method. A task that's canceled in this way transitions to the Canceled state, which the calling code can use to verify that the task responded to its cancellation request.

The first bullet point is easy to understand and justifies the final status of the canceled task (printTask) in the previous demonstration. In the next section, I'll show you the other approach where you will notice the final status as Canceled.

Alternative Approaches

Let us see the alternative ways of cancellations as well. In a similar context, developers often like to throw the OperationCanceledException exception.

Demonstration 2

To demonstrate this, let me update the task definition in the previous demonstration as follows (notice the key change in bold):

```
var printTask = Task.Run
  (
  () =>
  {
      // A loop that runs 100 times
      for (int i = 0; i < 100; i++)
      {
          // Approach-2
          if (token.IsCancellationRequested)
```

```
        {
            WriteLine("Cancelling the print activity.");
            // Do some cleanups, if required
            throw new OperationCanceledException(token);
        }

        WriteLine($"{i}");
        // Imposing the sleep to make some delay
        Thread.Sleep(500);
      }
  }, token
);
```

And execute the program again.

Output

Here is a sample output when I triggered the cancellation request by pressing "c" from my keyboard. Notice that in Demonstration 1, the final status of the task was RanToCompletion, but in this demonstration, it appears as Canceled.

```
Simple cancellation demonstration.
Enter c to cancel the task.
0
1
2
c
Raising the cancellation request.
Cancelling the print activity.
Caught: System.Threading.Tasks.TaskCanceledException, Message:
    A task was canceled.
The final status of printTask is: Canceled
End of the main thread.
```

Shortening The Code

Microsoft (see the online link https://learn.microsoft.com/en-us/
dotnet/api/system.threading.cancellationtoken.throwifcancellati
onrequested?view=net-8.0) says that the ThrowIfCancellationRequested
method is the functional equivalent of the following lines:

```
if (token.IsCancellationRequested)
    throw new OperationCanceledException(token);
```

It implies that you can use the ThrowIfCancellationRequested
method for the following two things:

- You can check whether a cancellation request is raised.

- Throw the OperationCanceledException exception
  when such a request is raised.

This is why you can shorten the code as follows:

```
var printTask = Task.Run
  (
    () =>
    {
        // A loop that runs 100 times
        for (int i = 0; i < 100; i++)
        {
            // Approach-3
            token.ThrowIfCancellationRequested();

            WriteLine($"{i}");
            // Imposing the sleep to make some delay
            Thread.Sleep(500);
        }
    }, token
  );
```

This is a common and widely used approach.

Note   Once you download the project Chapter5_Demo2, you can see the complete program. I've kept all the alternative approaches in the comments for your ready reference.

Q&A Session

Q5.2 In Demonstration 1, you simply did a soft exit and got the final task status as RanToCompletion, whereas in Demonstration 2, the final task status was canceled. I understand that this is a design decision, but I'd like to know your thoughts on them.

Normally, I'd like to follow the approach that is shown in Demonstration 2. This is because in an enterprise application, we normally deal with several tasks and we often need to understand the log/output. In those cases, I can go through the log to understand which task was canceled. But if you simply exit from the method without doing anything, there will be no such record left for you.

Q5.3 Before I cancel a task, I may need to do some cleanups (for example, to release a resource). How can I handle the situation if I use Approach-3?

In such a case, you can write something like the following:

```
if (token.IsCancellationRequested)
{
    // Do some cleanups, if required
    token.ThrowIfCancellationRequested();
}
```

Author's note: Microsoft suggests (see `https://learn.microsoft.com/` `en-us/dotnet/api/system.threading.cancellationtokensource.` `dispose?view=net-9.0`) the following:

> *Always call Dispose before you release your last reference to the CancellationTokenSource. Otherwise, the resources it is using will not be freed until the garbage collector calls the CancellationTokenSource object's Finalize method.*

Since the `CancellationTokenSource` class implements the IDisposable interface, once the demand is fulfilled, you can free up the resources by invoking the Dispose method. However, while freeing up resources, you need to be careful. To make the examples short and simple, I did not focus on explicit garbage collection mechanisms in these programs.

Additional Case Studies

The `OperationCanceledException` class has many overloaded constructors that take a different number of parameters. You can use any of them to initialize a new instance of `OperationCanceledException` as per your need. Here, I include some of them for your instant reference:

- `OperationCanceledException(CancellationToken)` – Initializes a new instance with a cancellation token (Demonstration 2 used this form)

- `OperationCanceledException(String)` – Initializes a new instance with a specified error message

- `OperationCanceledException()` – Initializes a new instance with the system-supplied error message

See that you can avoid passing a `CancellationToken` instance to initialize a new instance of `OperationCanceledException`, or you can instantiate it with a different token. In such cases, you get the final status as `Faulted` (instead of `Canceled`). Let us do some additional experiments:

Case Study 1: Changing the Task Definition

In Demonstration 2, let us update Approach-2 as follows (changes are in bold):

```
// Approach-2
if (token.IsCancellationRequested)
{
    WriteLine("Cancelling the print activity.");
    // Do some cleanups, if required
    // throw new OperationCanceledException(token);
    throw new OperationCanceledException("The operation is
        canceled.");
}
```

Execute the program again. Notice that the final status appears as Faulted but not Canceled. Here is a sample for you:

```
Simple cancellation demonstration.
Enter c to cancel the task.
0
1
2
c
Raising the cancellation request.
Cancelling the print activity.
Caught: System.OperationCanceledException, Message: The
operation is canceled.
The final status of printTask is: Faulted
End of the main thread.
```

Note   You can download the project Chapter5_Demo2_CaseStudy1
to see the complete program.

Q&A Session

**Q5.4 Why does the previous output show the final status Faulted
instead of Canceled?**

It is a design decision. The online link https://learn.microsoft.
com/en-us/dotnet/standard/parallel-programming/task-
cancellation states:

> *If the token's IsCancellationRequested property returns
> false or if the exception's token doesn't match the Task's
> token, the OperationCanceledException is treated like a
> normal exception, causing the Task to transition to the
> Faulted state. The presence of other exceptions will also cause
> the Task to transition to the Faulted state.*

Case Study 2: Changing the Caller

In Demonstration 2, let us use Wait(token) instead of Wait() in the try
block as follows:

```
// There is no change in the previous code
try
{
    // printTask.Wait();
    printTask.Wait(token);
}

// There is no change in the remaining code
```

Now, execute the program again. This time, you'll see that the OperationCanceledException is not wrapped inside the AggregateException. So, the catch block for the OperationCanceledException was necessary to handle the exception. Here is a sample output from my computer:

```
Simple cancellation demonstration.
Enter c to cancel the task.
0
1
2
c
Raising the cancellation request.
Operation canceled. Message: The operation was canceled.
The final status of printTask is: Running
End of the main thread.
```

Note   You can download the project Chapter5_Demo2_CaseStudy2 to see the complete program.

Q&A Session

Q5.5 Why does the previous output show the final status Running instead of Canceled or Faulted?

The Wait(token) differs from Wait(). In the case of Wait(token), the wait terminates if a cancellation token is canceled before the task is completed. In this case, the main thread exited early. To see the final status of the task, you can introduce the following code (shown in bold) in the following location:

```
// There is no change in the previous code.
```

```
// Wait till the task finishes the execution
while (!printTask.IsCompleted) { }
WriteLine($"The final status of printTask is: {printTask.
    Status}");
```

```
// There is no change in the remaining code.
```

Here is a sample output after this change:

```
Simple cancellation demonstration.
Enter c to cancel the task.
0
1
2
c
Raising the cancellation request.
Operation canceled. Message: The operation was canceled.
Cancelling the print activity.
The final status of printTask is: Faulted
End of the main thread.
```

POINTS TO NOTE

I want you to note the following points:

1. On a detailed examination, you'll see that Wait() can throw only AggregateException, whereas Wait(CancellationToken cancellationToken) is cancellable and can raise OperationCanceledException. If interested, you can see our

online discussion on this topic at https://stackoverflow.com/questions/77833724/why-the-catch-block-of-aggregateexception-was-not-sufficient-to-handle-cancellat/77833858#77833858.

2. To answer Q5.5, I have answered your question using the line while (!printTask.IsCompleted) { }. However, Microsoft suggests (see the online link https://learn.microsoft.com/en-us/dotnet/standard/parallel-programming/exception-handling-task-parallel-library) that you avoid this kind of polling in the production code as it is very inefficient.

3. In the previous output, you see the final status of the task as Faulted. It is because I used the line **throw new OperationCanceledException("The operation is canceled.");** in that demonstration. However, if you replace this line with **throw new OperationCanceledException(token)**; you can see the final status as **Canceled** but not **Faulted**.

Timeout Cancellation

You can initiate a cancellation request after a specified time. For example, for a typical network operation, you may not like to wait indefinitely. In such a case, your program can automatically initiate the cancellation request.

To implement the idea, you can use the line tokenSource.CancelAfter(2000); in the previous demonstration (Demonstration 2) as follows:

```
// There is no change in the previous code
var tokenSource = new CancellationTokenSource();
var token = tokenSource.Token;
```

```
tokenSource.CancelAfter(2000);
// There is no change in the remaining code
```

Now while executing the modified program, the program can automatically trigger the cancellation request after 2000 milliseconds.

Note   Since I am not changing the remaining code, this program can respond to user-initiated cancellations as well. In that case, the user needs to raise this request before this automatic cancellation triggers. In fact, it will wait for a user input before it closes the application. You can download the project **Chapter5_TimeoutCancellation** to see the complete program from the Apress website.

Monitoring Task Cancellation

In the output of some of the previous demonstrations (for example, see the output of Demonstration2, Chapter5_Demo2_CaseStudy1, or the answer to Q5.5), you saw the following line: `Cancelling the print activity`. I used this line to monitor the canceled task before the cancellation operation. Interestingly, there are alternative ways. Let us see some of them.

Using Register

You can subscribe to an event notification. For example, in the following code, I register a delegate that will be called when the token is canceled:

```
token.Register(
    () =>
    {
```

```
        WriteLine("Cancelling the print activity,
        [Using event subscription]");
        // Do something else, if you want
    }
);
```

Using WaitHandle.WaitOne

Let me show you one more approach that is relatively complicated compared to the previous one. However, this can also give you an idea about how to monitor task cancellation. The online link https://learn. microsoft.com/en-us/dotnet/api/system.threading.waithandle. waitone?view=net-8.0 describes WaitHandle's WaitOne method as follows:

> *Blocks the current thread until the current* WaitHandle *receives a signal.*

The WaitOne method has many overloads. In the upcoming demonstration, I'll show you the simplest form that does not require you to pass any argument. The basic idea is that the current thread will consider a token and wait until someone cancels this token. As soon as someone invokes the cancellation, the blocking function call will be released. This is why I can launch another task from the calling thread as follows:

```
Task.Run(
    () =>
    {
        token.WaitHandle.WaitOne();
        WriteLine("Cancelling the print activity.
         [Using WaitHandle]");
        // Do something else, if you want
    }
);
```

Notice that it is very similar to subscribing to an event notification, because here also you wait for the cancellation to occur. This is why I have written a similar statement in this code block.

Demonstration 3

It is time for another demonstration where I show you the discussed approaches to monitor the cancellation operation. Notice the key changes in bold:

```
using static System.Console;

WriteLine("Monitoring the cancellation operation.");

var tokenSource = new CancellationTokenSource();
var token = tokenSource.Token;

token.Register(
    () =>
    {
        WriteLine("Cancelling the print activity.[Using event
          subscription]");
        // Do something else, if you want
    }
  );

var printTask = Task.Run
 (
  () =>
  {
      // A loop that runs 100 times
      for (int i = 0; i < 100; i++)
      {
          // Approach-3
          token.ThrowIfCancellationRequested();
```

```
            WriteLine($"{i}");
            // Imposing the sleep to make some delay
            Thread.Sleep(500);
        }
    }, token
);
Task.Run(
    () =>
    {
        token.WaitHandle.WaitOne();
        WriteLine("Cancelling the print activity.[Using
         WaitHandle]");
        // Do something else, if you want
    }
);
WriteLine("Enter c to cancel the task.");
char ch = ReadKey().KeyChar;
if (ch.Equals('c'))
{
    WriteLine("\nTask cancellation requested.");
    tokenSource.Cancel();
}
// Wait till the task finishes the execution
while (!printTask.IsCompleted) { }
WriteLine($"The final status of printTask is: {printTask.Status}");
WriteLine("End of the main thread.");
```

Output

Here is one sample output. Notice the changes in bold.

```
Monitoring the cancellation operation.
Enter c to cancel the task.
0
1
2
c
Task cancellation requested.
Cancelling the print activity.[Using WaitHandle]
Cancelling the print activity.[Using event subscription]
The final status of printTask is: Canceled
End of the main thread.
```

Using Multiple Cancellation Tokens

An application can indeed be canceled due to various reasons. In such a case, you can use multiple tokens and provide the necessary logic. In this context, you can use the CreateLinkedTokenSource method. Let us see an example.

In the following demonstration, you'll see two different tokens as follows:

```
var normalCancellation = new CancellationTokenSource();
var tokenNormal = normalCancellation.Token;

var unexpectedCancellation = new CancellationTokenSource();
var tokenUnexpected = unexpectedCancellation.Token;
```

Once created, I pass them to the CreateLinkedTokenSource method as follows:

```
var compositeToken = CancellationTokenSource.
 CreateLinkedTokenSource(tokenNormal,tokenUnexpected);
```

The idea is that you can cause a cancellation using either normalCancellation or unexpectedCancellation.

You may note that the CreateLinkedTokenSource method has different overloads and you can pass more tokens if required. Remember that the core idea is the same: you can cancel any of these tokens to make the final task status Canceled.

Demonstration 4

In the following program, a user can trigger a normal cancellation. However, you can also observe an unexpected/emergency cancellation. To mimic an emergency cancellation, I rely on a random number generator. If the random number is 5, the unexpected cancellation will be triggered. Here is the complete program to demonstrate the idea:

```
using static System.Console;

WriteLine("Monitoring the cancellation operation.");

var normalCancellation = new CancellationTokenSource();
var tokenNormal = normalCancellation.Token;

var unexpectedCancellation = new CancellationTokenSource();
var tokenUnexpected = unexpectedCancellation.Token;

tokenNormal.Register(
    () =>
    {
        WriteLine("Processing a normal cancellation.");
```

```
        // Do something else, if you want
    }
  );

tokenUnexpected.Register(
    () =>
    {
        WriteLine("Processing an unexpected cancellation.");
        // Do something else, if you want
    }
  );

var compositeToken = CancellationTokenSource.
CreateLinkedTokenSource(
 tokenNormal,
 tokenUnexpected
);

var printTask = Task.Run
 (
  () =>
  {
      // A loop that runs 100 times
      for (int i = 0; i < 100; i++)
      {
          compositeToken.Token.ThrowIfCancellationRequested();
          WriteLine($"{i}");
          // Imposing sleep to make some delay
          Thread.Sleep(500);
      }
  }, compositeToken.Token
);
```

```
int random = new Random().Next(1, 6);
// A dummy logic to mimic an emergency cancellation
if (random == 5)
    unexpectedCancellation.Cancel();
else
{
  WriteLine("Enter a key (type c for a normal cancellation)");
  char ch = ReadKey().KeyChar;
  if (ch.Equals('c'))
  {
    WriteLine("\nTask cancellation requested.");
    normalCancellation.Cancel();
  }
}

// Wait till the task finishes the execution
while (!printTask.IsCompleted) { }
WriteLine($"The final status of printTask is: {printTask.
  Status}");
WriteLine("End of the main thread.");
```

Output

Here is a sample output when a user pressed "c" to initiate a normal cancellation:

```
Monitoring the cancellation operation.
Enter a key (type c for a normal cancellation)
0
1
2
c
Task cancellation requested.
```

Processing a normal cancellation.
The final status of printTask is: Canceled
End of the main thread.

Here is another sample output when an emergency cancellation was triggered automatically:

Monitoring the cancellation operation.
Processing an unexpected cancellation.
The final status of printTask is: Canceled
End of the main thread.

Summary

Cancellation is an essential mechanism in task programming. However, instead of abruptly stopping a task, you make a cooperative model where the task and the calling code (that initiates the cancellation) can work together to maintain the health of your application. This chapter discussed this topic and answered the following questions:

- How can you support user-initiated cancellations?

- How can you support the timeout cancellations?

- How can you monitor cancellations in your application?

- How can you use multiple cancellation tokens in your application?

Exercises

Check your understanding by attempting the following exercises:

REMINDER

As said before, you can safely assume that all other necessary namespaces are available for these code segments. The same comment applies to all exercises in this book as well.

E5.1 If you execute the following code, can you predict the output?

```
using static System.Console;

var tokenSource = new CancellationTokenSource();
var token = tokenSource.Token;
var printTask = Task.Run
 (
   () =>
   {
       int i = 0;
       while (i != 10)
       {
           if (token.IsCancellationRequested)
           {
               WriteLine("Cancelling the print activity.");
               return;
           }
           // Do some work, if required.
           Thread.Sleep(1000);
           i++;
       }
```

```
    }, token
);
```

```
Thread.Sleep(500);
WriteLine("The cancellation is initiated.");
tokenSource.Cancel();
// Wait till the task finishes the execution
while (!printTask.IsCompleted) { }
WriteLine($"The final status of printTask is: {printTask.Status}");
WriteLine("End of the main thread.");
```

E5.2 In the previous exercise, replace the following code segment:

```
if (token.IsCancellationRequested)
{
    WriteLine("Cancelling the print activity.");
    return;
}
```

with the following line:

```
token.ThrowIfCancellationRequested();
```

Will there be any change in the output?

E5.3 The following program creates a parent task and a nested task. It also allows you to cancel these tasks if you press "c" from the keyboard. Check whether you can predict the output.

```
using static System.Console;
```

```
WriteLine("Exercise 5.3");
var tokenSource = new CancellationTokenSource();
var token = tokenSource.Token;
```

```
Task child = null;
var parent = Task.Factory.StartNew(
```

```
() =>
{
    Thread.Sleep(1000);
    if (token.IsCancellationRequested)
    {
        WriteLine( "The cancellation request is raised too early.");
        token.ThrowIfCancellationRequested();
    }
    WriteLine("The parent task is running.");
    // Creating a nested task
    child = Task.Factory.StartNew(
      () =>
      {
          WriteLine("The child task has started.");
          for (int i = 0; i < 10; i++)
          {
              token.ThrowIfCancellationRequested();
              WriteLine($"\tThe nested task prints:{i} ");
              Thread.Sleep(200);
          }
          return "The child task has finished too";
      },
      token,
      TaskCreationOptions.AttachedToParent,
      TaskScheduler.Default);
    child.Wait(token);
},token);
WriteLine("Enter c to cancel the nested task.");
char ch = ReadKey().KeyChar;
```

```csharp
if (ch.Equals('c'))
{
    WriteLine("\nTask cancellation requested.");
    tokenSource.Cancel();
}
try
{
    parent.Wait();
}
catch (AggregateException ae)
{
    foreach (Exception e in ae.InnerExceptions)
    {
        WriteLine($"Caught error: {e.Message}");
    }
}
WriteLine($"The current state of the parent task: {parent.
    Status}");
string childStatus = child != null ? child.Status.ToString() :
    "not created";
WriteLine($"The current state of the child task: {childStatus}");
WriteLine("End of the main thread.");
```

E5.4 State True/False:

i)   The CancellationTokenSource is a class that
     implements the IDisposable interface.

ii) The Token property of the CancellationTokenSource
     class is used to generate the CancellationToken
     instance.

E5.5 In Chapter 3, you solved the exercise E3.2. Since you have learned about implementing exception and cancellation scenarios, can you solve that exercise considering these scenarios?

Solutions to Exercises

Here is a sample solution set for the exercises in this chapter.

E5.1

The program will automatically initiate a cancellation. Here is a possible output (notice that the task status is RanToCompletion but not Canceled):

```
The cancellation is initiated.
Cancelling the print activity.
The final status of printTask is: RanToCompletion
End of the main thread.
```

E5.2

This time the final task status should appear as Canceled. Here is a sample output:

```
The cancellation is initiated.
The final status of printTask is: Canceled
End of the main thread.
```

E5.3

You already know that this program creates a parent task and a nested task. It also lets you cancel the nested task if you press "c" quickly. As a result, depending on the situation, you may see a different output. For example, if you do not initiate a cancellation and press the Enter key at the end, you can see the following output:

```
Exercise 5.3
Enter c to cancel the nested task.
```

```
The parent task is running.
The child task has started.
         The nested task prints:0
         The nested task prints:1
         The nested task prints:2
         The nested task prints:3
         The nested task prints:4
         The nested task prints:5
         The nested task prints:6
         The nested task prints:7
         The nested task prints:8
         The nested task prints:9
The current state of the parent task: RanToCompletion
The current state of the child task: RanToCompletion
End of the main thread.
```

On the other hand, depending on the time of cancellation, you can get different outputs. For example, if you press **c** almost at the beginning of the application, you can see the following:

```
Exercise 5.3
Enter c to cancel the nested task.
c
Task cancellation requested.
```
The cancellation request is raised too early.
```
Caught error: A task was canceled.
The current state of the parent task: Canceled
The current state of the child task: not created
End of the main thread.
```

Otherwise, you may see a normal cancellation that is something like the following:

Exercise 5.3
Enter c to cancel the nested task.
The parent task is running.
The child task has started.
        The nested task prints:0
        The nested task prints:1
c
Task cancellation requested.
Caught error: A task was canceled.
The current state of the parent task: Canceled
The current state of the child task: Canceled
End of the main thread.

E5.4

The answers are shown inline in bold:

   i)   The CancellationTokenSource is a class that
        implements the IDisposable interface. [**True**]

   ii) The Token property of the CancellationTokenSource
        class is used to generate the CancellationToken
        instance. [**True**]

E5.5

I leave this exercise to you now. Good luck!

Additional note: This time onward, while solving the exercises, you can
exercise applying cancellation and exception mechanisms. The same
comment applies to the exercises that you solved in the previous chapters.

CHAPTER 6

Bonus

This chapter discusses some additional topics on task programming.

Progress Reporting

You can see the progress status while updating the operating system or installing a new version of Visual Studio on a computer. Let's see whether you can create an application with a similar feature using task programming.

Understanding the Need

Consider that you are processing many different records. To mimic the real world, let us further assume that the processing time of these records varies as well. Since the operation can be time-consuming, you do not want to block the main thread. Instead, you decide to complete it through a background task.

Demonstration 1

However, while processing those records, if you do not show the progress status, the user can be confused. To make things simple, let's see a sample demonstration that deals with only five records as follows:

```
using static System.Console;

WriteLine("The main thread is initiating a task to process some
    records.");
var recordProcessingTask = Task.Run(ProcessRecords);
```

© Vaskaran Sarcar 2025
V. Sarcar, *Task Programming in C# and .NET*, Apress Pocket Guides,
https://doi.org/10.1007/979-8-8688-1279-8_6

```
WriteLine("The main thread is doing other work now.");
recordProcessingTask.Wait();

static void ProcessRecords()
{
    WriteLine($"Starts processing the records...");
    for (int i = 1; i <= 5; i++)
    {
        // Varying the delay
        Thread.Sleep(i * 500);
    }
    WriteLine("All the records are processed.");
}
```

Output

Here is a sample output that should not cause any surprise for you:

```
The main thread is initiating a task to process some records.
The main thread is doing other work now.
Starts processing the records...
All the records are processed.
```

Analysis

However, you'll see that the line "All the records are processed." has appeared after a significant amount of time. From a user perspective, it is a confusing behavior because after you see the line "Starts processing the records...", you do not know what is happening in the background. **You understand that progress reporting can help you in a similar context, particularly when you execute a long-running task.**

Now, the question is: how can you report the progress? Well, it's up to you. For example, you may simply try to print which record is currently under process, or you may display the progress in terms of percentage by printing something like "completed processing:60%". In the upcoming example, I'd like to show you a sample demonstration using the built-in constructs for progress reporting. Let's start discussion about it.

There is an interface, called IProgress, in the System namespace. It contains a method, called Report, that can help you display the progress. Visual Studio reveals its look as follows:

```
public interface IProgress<in T>
{
    //
    // Summary:
    //      Reports a progress update.
    //
    // Parameters:
    //   value:
    //      The value of the updated progress.
    void Report(T value);
}
```

Using this interface, you can create a custom implementation to report progress.

You may note that there is also a built-in class, called Progress<T>, that already implements the IProgress interface. So, you can use this class to serve your purpose. This class exposes a ProgressChanged event that can be raised with every progress update sent from the asynchronous code.

There is an alternative option. Before you see this option, let me tell you that this Progress class has two constructors and one of them is as follows:

```
public Progress(Action<T> handler);
```

This gives you a clue that you can pass a delegate as a parameter to the constructor of the Progress class. **This delegate effectively acts as an event handler that you can use to report the progress.** Let me update the previous code to demonstrate how it works.

First, I changed the ProcessRecords function, so that it can accept IProgress<int> as a parameter. Let us see the modified function with the key changes in bold.

POINTS TO NOTE

I want you to note the following points:

- To make things simple, I have considered the int parameter. However, you can choose other types as well.

- Since there are five records, after processing a record, I increase the progress percentage by 20%.

```
static void ProcessRecords(IProgress<int> progress)
{
    WriteLine($"Starts processing the records...");
    int progressPercentage = 0;
    for (int i = 1; i <=5; i++)
    {
        // Varying the delay
        Thread.Sleep(i * 500);
        progressPercentage += 20;
        progress.Report(progressPercentage);
    }
    WriteLine("All the records are processed.");
}
```

To use this modified function, I needed to update the calling code as well. So, I replace the following line:

```
var recordProcessingTask = Task.Run(ProcessRecords);
```

with the following lines:

```
IProgress<int> reportProgress = new Progress<int>(
  i => WriteLine($"Completed: {i}%")
);
var recordProcessingTask = Task.Run(() => ProcessRecords(report
    Progress));
```

You can see that the Progress<int> constructor now accepts a delegate that will receive the progress data as a parameter. It will be executed every time a progress report is sent.

Demonstration 2

Let us see the modified demonstration now:

```
using static System.Console;
WriteLine("The main thread is initiating a task to process some
    records.");

IProgress<int> reportProgress = new Progress<int>(
 i => WriteLine($"Completed: {i}%")
);

var recordProcessingTask = Task.Run(() => ProcessRecords(report
    Progress));
WriteLine("The main thread is doing other work now.");
recordProcessingTask.Wait();

// The ProcessRecords function is placed here. It is not shown
// again to avoid repetition.
```

Note   Download Chapter6_Demo2 project to see the complete demonstration.

Output

Here is a sample output:

```
The main thread is initiating a task to process some records.
The main thread is doing other work now.
Starts processing the records...
Completed: 20%
Completed: 40%
Completed: 60%
Completed: 80%
All the records are processed.
Completed: 100%
```

You can see that the program can successfully print the update status.

Creating and Running Tasks Implicitly

At a high level, TPL has the following parts:

- The task parallelism constructs

- The Parallel class

TPL supports **data parallelism** through the Parallel class. You can exercise the parallel version of the for loop (using **Parallel. For**) and foreach loop using this class (using **Parallel.ForEach**). The detailed discussion on the Parallel class is beyond the scope of this book. However, I'd like to mention that the Parallel class has a useful method, called Invoke, that helps you create multiple tasks that can run concurrently.

Author's note: Since the first part (i.e., the task parallelism constructs) is already covered in this book, I'm not talking about it in this section.

Using Parallel.Invoke

The online link https://learn.microsoft.com/en-us/previous-versions/msp-n-p/ff963549(v=pandp.10)?redirectedfrom=MSDN states:

> *Parallel.Invoke is the simplest expression of the parallel task pattern. It creates new parallel tasks for each delegate method that is in its **params** array argument list. The **Invoke** method returns when all the tasks are finished.*

At the time of this writing, there are two overloads for the parallel Invoke method. Let me consider the simplest one that has the following look:

```
public static void Invoke (params Action[] actions);
```

You understand that while using this method, you can pass a variable number of Action instances to the Invoke method. Let me create three such instances and pass them in the following program.

Demonstration 3

Here is the complete demonstration.

```
using static System.Console;

#region Parallel.Invoke
WriteLine("Using Parallel.Invoke method.");
Action greet = new(() => WriteLine($"Task {Task.CurrentId}
    says: Hello reader!"));
```

```
Action printMsg = new(() => WriteLine($"Task {Task.CurrentId}
    says: This is a beautiful day."));
Action ask = new(() => WriteLine($"Task {Task.CurrentId} says:
    How are you?"));
Parallel.Invoke(greet, printMsg, ask);
WriteLine("End Parallel.Invoke");
#endregion
```

Output

Here is a sample output:

```
Using Parallel.Invoke method.
Task 3 says: Hello reader!
Task 1 says: This is a beautiful day.
Task 2 says: How are you?
End Parallel.Invoke
```

Additional Suggestions

Before I finish this section, I have the following suggestions for you:

- To have greater control over task executions, you'd like to create and execute tasks explicitly.

- Once you finish this book and learn more about asynchronous programming, you can read the online post comparing these approaches at https://devblogs.microsoft.com/pfxteam/task-run-vs-task-factory-startnew/. Though the article was written a long time back, it is still useful. However, to understand this material, you need to be familiar with async and await keywords.

Q&A Session

Q6.1 I can see that task 2 finishes after task 3 in the previous output. Is this an expected behavior? I can also see that you did not wait for the tasks to be finished. Is this OK?

Yes. The online link https://learn.microsoft.com/en-us/dotnet/api/system.threading.tasks.parallel.invoke?view=net-9.0 states:

> *This method can be used to execute a set of operations, potentially in parallel. No guarantees are made about the order in which the operations execute or whether they execute in parallel. This method does not return until each of the provided operations has completed, regardless of whether completion occurs due to normal or exceptional termination.*

Q6.2 It appears to me that I could create separate tasks and wait for them to finish their executions instead of using Parallel.Invoke. Is this correct?

Nice observation. The online link https://learn.microsoft.com/en-us/previous-versions/msp-n-p/ff963549(v=pandp.10)?redirected from=MSDN confirms that by saying the following:

> *Internally, Parallel.Invoke creates new tasks and waits for them. It uses methods of the Task class to do this.*

If you study the mentioned link, you will understand that I could write an equivalent program as follows:

```
using static System.Console;

Task  greet2 = Task.Factory.StartNew(
() => WriteLine($"Task {Task.CurrentId} says: Hello reader!"));

Task printMsg2 = Task.Factory.StartNew(
() => WriteLine($"Task {Task.CurrentId} says: This is a
    beautiful day."));
```

```
Task ask2 = Task.Factory.StartNew(
() => WriteLine($"Task {Task.CurrentId} says: How are you?"));

Task.WaitAll(greet2, printMsg2, ask2);
```

However, notice that when you work with a large number of delegates, creating separate tasks for each of those delegates and managing them is not a good idea. The use of `Parallel.Invoke` can give you the relief! It will work efficiently in those cases as well.

Q6.3 How does the data parallelism differ from the task parallelism?

Microsoft (`https://learn.microsoft.com/en-us/previous-versions/msp-n-p/ff963549(v=pandp.10)?redirectedfrom=MSDN`) summarizes the difference nicely by saying the following:

> *Data parallelism and task parallelism are two ends of a spectrum. Data parallelism occurs when a single operation is applied to many inputs. Task parallelism uses multiple operations, each with its own input.*

Precomputed Tasks

One of the primary benefits of performing asynchronous operations is faster executions. However, despite your best efforts, some of the operations are indeed time-consuming. To tackle such a situation, you can use the caching mechanism. Let's explore it in more detail.

Without Caching

The following program exercises a time-consuming method, named `TimeConsumingMethod`. Each time you call this method, you need to wait more than three seconds to get a random number. Let us exercise a program that invokes this method multiple times.

Demonstration 4

Here is a sample demonstration.

```
using System.Diagnostics;
using static System.Console;

Stopwatch stopwatch = Stopwatch.StartNew();
WriteLine(Sample.TimeConsumingMethod().Result);
stopwatch.Stop();
WriteLine($"Elapsed time: {stopwatch.ElapsedMilliseconds}
    milliseconds");

stopwatch.Restart();
// Subsequent calls
WriteLine(Sample.TimeConsumingMethod().Result);
stopwatch.Stop();
WriteLine($"Elapsed time: {stopwatch.ElapsedMilliseconds}
    milliseconds");
class Sample
{
    static int flagValue = 0;
    public static Task<int> TimeConsumingMethod()
    {
        return Task.Run(
            () =>
            {
                WriteLine("Forming the value...");
                // Simulating a delay before forming the value
                Thread.Sleep(3000);
                flagValue = new Random().Next(0, 100);
                return flagValue;
            }
```

```
        );
    }
}
```

Output

Here is a sample output:

```
Forming the value...
87
Elapsed time: 3092 milliseconds
Forming the value...
45
Elapsed time: 3017 milliseconds
```

Analysis

You can see that every time you invoke the time-consuming method, it takes more than three seconds to return a number.

Applying Caching Mechanism

You can apply the caching mechanism to improve the program. The idea is that once the value is formed, you'll hold the value in the cache. As a result, the next time a user calls the method, you can supply the cached value to him.

You can use Task.FromResult method in this context. This method will help you return a finished Task<TResult> object that holds the provided value as its Result property. In particular, this method is helpful when you perform an asynchronous operation that returns a Task<TResult> object, and the result of that object is already available.

Demonstration 5

Let us modify the time-consuming method in the Sample class as follows:

```
// There is no other change in the previous code
class Sample
{
    static bool cacheFormed;
    static int flagValue = 0;
    public static Task<int> TimeConsumingMethod()
    {
        return Task.Run(() =>
        {
            if (!cacheFormed)
            {
                WriteLine("First call: forming the value…");
                // Simulating a delay before forming the value
                Thread.Sleep(3000);
                flagValue = new Random().Next(0, 100);
                cacheFormed = true;
            }
            else
            {
                WriteLine("Subsequent call(s): getting the value
                    from the cache.");
                Task.FromResult(flagValue);
            }
            return flagValue;
        }
    );
    }
}
```

Output

Here is a sample output:

```
First call: forming the value...
42
Elapsed time: 3026 milliseconds
Subsequent call(s): getting the value from the cache.
42
Elapsed time: 1 milliseconds
```

Analysis

You can see that the caching mechanism improved response time significantly in the subsequent calls.

Q&A Session

Q6.4 Can you give me a real-world example where I can use precomputed tasks?

Suppose, there is an application where a user provides a URL. Then the application starts downloading the data from that URL for further processing. In this case, to avoid repeated downloads, you can store the URL and the corresponding data in a cache.

Using TaskCompletionSource

You have seen that tasks can help you perform background work. They are also useful for managing work items like performing continuation works, managing child tasks, or handling exceptions. However, in some cases, you may need to have more control over the tasks. The TaskCompletionSource<TResult> class can be useful in those scenarios. Let's explore its usage.

The `TaskCompletionSource<TResult>` class allows you to create a task out of any operation that will be completed in the future. In the online link `https://learn.microsoft.com/en-us/dotnet/api/system.threading.tasks.taskcompletionsource-1?view=net-8.0` Microsoft describes this class as follows:

> *Represents the producer side of a Task<TResult> unbound to a delegate, providing access to the consumer side through the Task property.*

More specifically, behind the scenes, using this class, you get a "slave" task that you can manually drive for completion. It can be ideal for such type of I/O bound work where you reap all the benefits of using a task without blocking the calling thread.

How to Use?

Now the question is: how to use this class? First, you need to instantiate it. Once you instantiate this class, you will get some built-in methods that can serve your purpose. Here is a sample screenshot from Visual Studio that shows the details of this class (see Figure 6-1).

```
using System.Collections.Generic;

namespace System.Threading.Tasks
{
    public class TaskCompletionSource<TResult>
    {
        public TaskCompletionSource();
        public TaskCompletionSource(object? state);
        public TaskCompletionSource(TaskCreationOptions creationOptions);
        public TaskCompletionSource(object? state, TaskCreationOptions creationOptions);

        public Task<TResult> Task { get; }

        public void SetCanceled();
        public void SetCanceled(CancellationToken cancellationToken);
        public void SetException(IEnumerable<Exception> exceptions);
        public void SetException(Exception exception);
        public void SetResult(TResult result);
        public bool TrySetCanceled();
        public bool TrySetCanceled(CancellationToken cancellationToken);
        public bool TrySetException(IEnumerable<Exception> exceptions);
        public bool TrySetException(Exception exception);
        public bool TrySetResult(TResult result);
    }
}
```

Figure 6-1. The TaskCompletionSource class details

From this screenshot, you can see that the method names start either with "Set" or "TrySet". The first category returns void, but the second category returns bool. You can note the following points about these methods:

- When you call any of these methods, the task moves into any of the final states: RanToCompletion, Faulted, or Canceled.

- You should call the first category (i.e., where the method names start with the word "Set") exactly once; otherwise, you'll see exceptions. (The answer to Q6.5 discusses more on this.)

Demonstration 6

Let's see a demonstration. To understand the following program, read the following points:

- At the beginning of the program, I created an instance of TaskCompletionSource<string> class, called tcs. As a result, I can use its Task property in a later stage.

- The user of this application can get the details of the background activity by entering the character "**y**". If the user enters any other character, the program completes execution without showing the details.

Let us see the complete program now:

```
using static System.Console;

WriteLine($"The TaskCompletionSource demo.");
TaskCompletionSource<string> tcs = new();
Task<string> collectInfoTask = tcs.Task;

// Starting a background task that will complete the work
var backgroundTask = Task.Run(
() =>
{
    WriteLine("Monitoring the activity before setting the result.");
    // Imposing some forced delay before setting the
    // result to mimic real-world
    Thread.Sleep(3000);
    bool isSuccess = tcs.TrySetResult("Everything went well.");
    if (isSuccess)
    {
        WriteLine("\nThe result is set successfully.");
    }
});
```

```
WriteLine("\nEnter a key (if interested, press 'y' to get the
    details).");
var input = ReadKey();
if (input.KeyChar == 'y')
{
    WriteLine($"\nReceived: {collectInfoTask.Result}");
}
WriteLine("\nThank you!");
```

Output

Here are some sample outputs.

Case 1 (the user opts for the detail):

```
The TaskCompletionSource demo.

Enter a key (if interested, press 'y' to get the details).
Monitoring the activity before setting the result.
y
The result is set successfully.

Received: Everything went well.

Thank you!
```

Case 2 (the user does not opt for the detail and types "n"):

```
The TaskCompletionSource demo.

Enter a key (if interested, press 'y' to get the details).
Monitoring the activity before setting the result.
n
Thank you!
```

Q&A Session

Q6.5 Before Demonstration 6, you said the following: "You should call the first category (i.e., where the method names start with the word "Set") exactly once; otherwise, you'll see exceptions." Can you please elaborate?

If you use the following version of the backgroundTask :

```
var backgroundTask = Task.Run(
() =>
{
    WriteLine("Monitoring the activity before setting the
    result.");
    // Imposing some forced delay before setting the
    // result to mimic real-world
    Thread.Sleep(3000);
    tcs.SetResult("Everything went well.");
    //// The following line will cause an exception now
    //tcs.SetResult("The result is set for the second time.");
});
```

You can see an identical output. Let's try to set the result one more time as follows:

```
// There is no change in the previous code
tcs.SetResult("Everything went well.");
// The following line will cause an exception now
tcs.SetResult("The result is set for the second time.");
// There is no change in the remaining code
```

Now, wait for this task to finish (e.g., using the line backgroundTask. Wait(); in the client code); you will see the following exception in the final output:

```
Unhandled exception. System.AggregateException: One or more
errors occurred. (An attempt was made to transition a task to a
final state when it had already completed.)
// The remaining details are not shown
```

Note   To see a sample implementation, you can download the
Chapter6_Demo6_TCS_Q&A project, for your experimentation/
reference from the Apress website.

To avoid this kind of error, I prefer to use the TrySetResult method
instead of the SetResult method. The reason is obvious: it returns a
Boolean, i.e., either true or false, but not an exception.

**Q6.6 Can you give a real-world example where I can benefit from using
the TaskCompletionSource class?**

Consider an event-based application where a user needs to provide some
credentials. Let's assume that once these credentials are entered, an event is
raised. If the user provides valid credentials, the application stores his current
activity in a database. Otherwise, the application can raise an exception, and
the error details can be popped up on the screen. You can consider using the
TaskCompletionSource<TResult> class to make such an application.

Summary

This chapter provides some supplementary material that can help you in
task programming. Upon completion of this chapter, you can answer the
following questions:

- How can you report progress while executing a long-
  running task?

- How can you create tasks implicitly?

- IIow can you benefit from a precomputed task?

- How can `TaskCompletionSource` class help you manage an I/O-bound task?

Exercises

Check your understanding by attempting the following exercises:

REMINDER

As said before, you can safely assume that all other necessary namespaces are available for these code segments. The same comment applies to all exercises in this book as well.

E6.1 If you execute the following code, can you predict the output?

```
using static System.Console;
TaskCompletionSource<int> tcs = new();
int value = 10;
var task1=Task.Run(() => value++);
task1.Wait();
var task2=Task.Run(() =>
{
    tcs.SetResult(value*10);
}
);
WriteLine($"The final result is: {tcs.Task.Result}");
```

E6.2 Can you predict the following output of the following program?

```
using static System.Console;
var task = Task.Run(() => "Thanks God!");
string msg = string.Concat( task.Result, " What a beautiful
    day!") ;
var task2 = Task.FromResult(msg);
WriteLine(task2.Result);
```

E6.3 Can you predict the following output of the following program?

```
using static System.Console;
try
{
    Action greet = new(() => WriteLine($"Hello reader!"));
    Action raiseError = new(
        () => throw new Exception("There is a problem."));
    Parallel.Invoke(greet, raiseError);
}
catch (AggregateException ae)
{
    foreach (Exception ex in ae.InnerExceptions)
    {
        WriteLine(ex.Message);
    }
}
```

Solutions to Exercises

Here is the solution set for the exercises in this chapter.

E6.1

You should see the following output:

```
The final result is: 110
```

[**Clue**: Notice that task1 updates the initial value to 11, but task2 further sets it as 11*10=110. The Wait statement was placed to preserve the order of evaluation.]

E6.2

You should see the following output:

```
Thanks God! What a beautiful day!
```

E6.3

Here is the output:

```
Hello reader!
There is a problem.
```

Author's note: This output is predictable. Why? You'll always see the error message "There is a problem" after the line "Hello reader!". The online link https://learn.microsoft.com/en-us/previous-versions/msp-n-p/ff963549(v=pandp.10)?redirectedfrom=MSDN confirms that by saying the following:

> *Any exceptions that occur during the execution of Parallel. Invoke are **deferred and rethrown when all tasks finish**. All exceptions are rethrown as inner exceptions of an AggregateException instance.*

APPENDIX A

What's Next?

Task programming is the foundation of modern-day asynchronous programming. I hope that after completing this book, you get a fair idea about it. Now I suggest you read the related topics from other books, articles, or blogs. Most importantly, you should keep experimenting with new code and learn more. We all know that practice makes a man perfect.

The next step is exercising `async` and `await` keywords in your program. A dedicated pocketbook in this series will cover that topic. You may note that I wrote a book on parallel programming (*Parallel Programming with C# and .NET* (Apress, 2024)) which covers that topic as well. If you like this book, you may want to learn more about asynchronous and parallel programming from that book.

I always keep coding, practicing programs, and learning from others. This is why in the following recommended list, you will see a few more books, courses, and articles from which I got many new insights. I believe that they will be equally effective for you. You can learn more from these materials (or their updated editions) as well.

Books

Here is my recommended list of books:

- *C# 12 in a Nutshell* by Joseph Albahari (O'Reilly Media, first edition, December 2023)

© Vaskaran Sarcar 2025
V. Sarcar, *Task Programming in C# and .NET*, Apress Pocket Guides,
https://doi.org/10.1007/979-8-8688-1279-8

- *Pro .NET 4 Parallel Programming in C#* by Adam Freeman (Apress, first edition May 2010)

- *Parallel Programming with C# and .NET* (Apress, first edition, September 2024)

In this list of books, the first one is my favorite. The second one is quite old but still helpful. I'd also like to add that I have learned many things from Stephen Cleary's blogs/articles. However, I have not read his book on this topic yet. If interested, you may look at the following one as well:

- *Concurrency in C# Cookbook: Asynchronous, Parallel, and Multithreaded Programming* (O'Reilly Media; second edition (October 2019)

Courses

The following list includes helpful online courses. These cover a wide number of topics. At the time of this writing, none of them are free. However, you may get a promotional discount occasionally on these courses.

- `https://www.udemy.com/course/parallel-dotnet/learn/lecture/5645430#overview`

- `https://www.udemy.com/course/parallel-csharp/learn/lecture/11126093#overview`

Other Resources

In each chapter, you have seen various online resources in the discussions and the "Q&A Sessions." You can have a detailed look at those resources to learn more about them.

APPENDIX B

Other Books by the Author

The following list includes other Apress books by the author:

- *Parallel Programming with C# and .NET* (Apress, 2024)

- *Introducing Functional Programming Using C#* (Apress, 2023)

- *Simple and Efficient Programming in C# Second Edition* (Apress, 2022)

- *Test Your Skills in C# Programming* (Apress, 2022)

- *Java Design Patterns Third Edition* (Apress, 2022)

- *Simple and Efficient Programming in C#* (Apress, 2021)

- *Design Patterns in C# Second Edition* (Apress, 2020)

- *Getting Started with Advanced C#* (Apress, 2020)

- *Interactive Object-Oriented Programming in Java Second Edition* (Apress, 2019)

- *Java Design Patterns Second Edition* (Apress, 2019)

© Vaskaran Sarcar 2025
V. Sarcar, *Task Programming in C# and .NET*, Apress Pocket Guides,
https://doi.org/10.1007/979-8-8688-1279-8

- *Design Patterns in C#* (Apress, 2018)

- *Interactive C#* (Apress, 2017)

- *Interactive Object-Oriented Programming in Java* (Apress, 2016)

- *Java Design Patterns* (Apress, 2016)

The following list includes his non-Apress books:

- *Python Bookcamp* (Amazon, 2021)

- *Operating System: Computer Science Interview Series* (Createspace, 2014)

To learn more about these books, you can refer to any of the following links:

- https://amazon.com/author/vaskaran_sarcar

- https://link.springer.com/search?newsearch=true &query=vaskaran+sarcar&content-type=book&dateFr om=&dateTo=&sortBy=newestFirst

Index

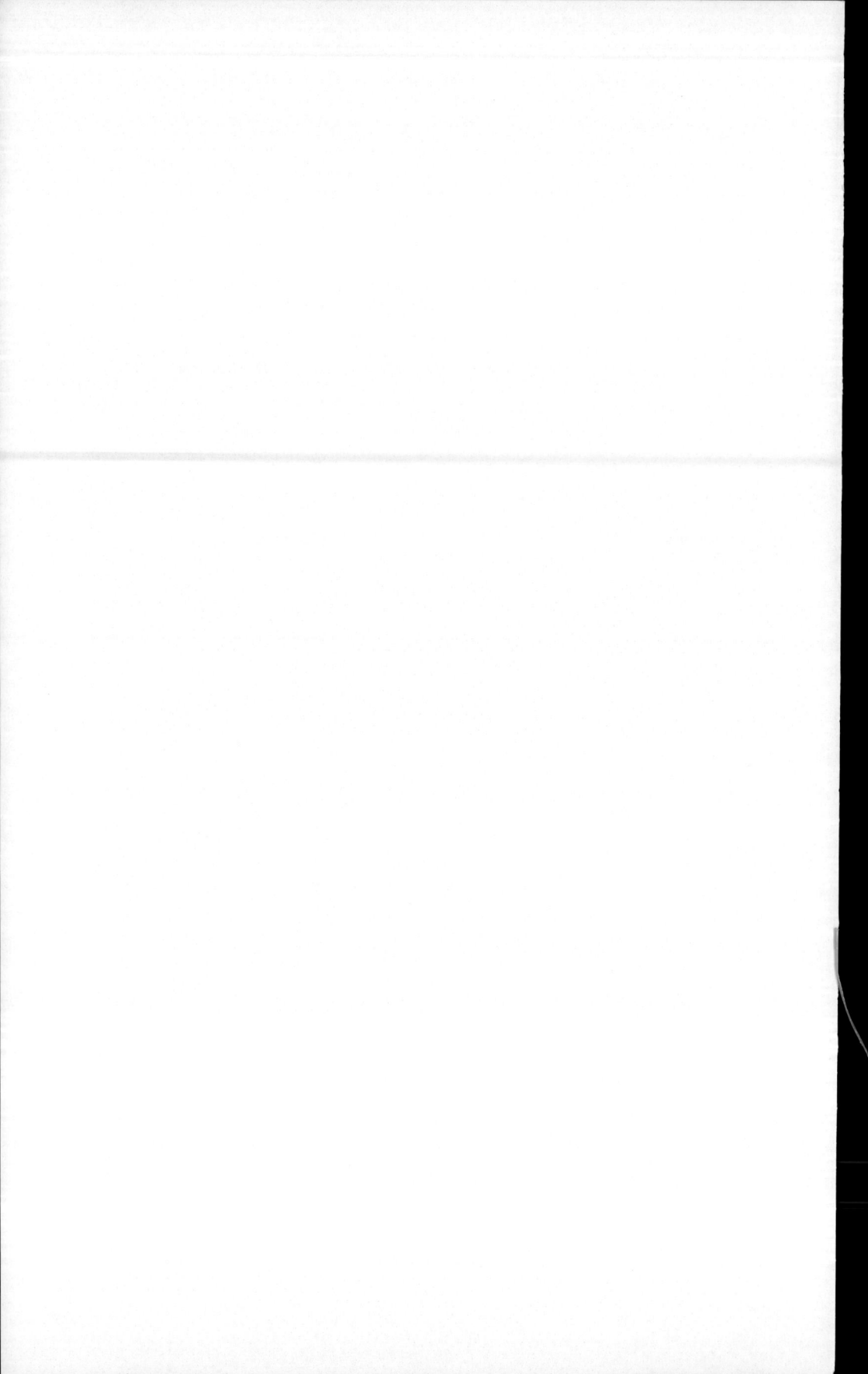